THE PRACTICAL WAY
TO
A BETTER MEMORY

THE PRACTICAL WAY

TO

A Better Memory

By BRUNO FURST

Director of the School of Memory and Concentration
and author of "You *Can* Remember!"
and "Stop Forgetting"

R. & W. HEAP (PUBLISHING) CO. LTD.
MARPLE, CHESHIRE

PRINTED IN GREAT BRITAIN BY
REDWOOD BOOKS, TROWBRIDGE, WILTSHIRE

ACKNOWLEDGMENTS

I wish to acknowledge with thanks my indebtedness to Mrs. Hortense Dillon, Mr. Samuel Ebenstein, Mrs. Virginia E. Flynn, Mr. Lawrence Scheewe and Mr. Edwin C. Silvey for their friendly assistance in gathering the material for this work. Also to Miss Elinore Denniston and Miss Lorna Dietz for help in putting it into its present form.

Miss Bert Warter did the drawings.

THE AUTHOR

TO
LOTTE FURST

CONTENTS

PART ONE

The Cultivation of Memory

CONTENTS

PART TWO

The Art of Public Address

PART ONE

THE CULTIVATION OF MEMORY

CHAPTER I

THE GOAL AHEAD

YOU are reading this book because you wish to develop all the potentialities of your mind, to acquire greater mental power, an increased ability to concentrate, more self-confidence. You have found that your memory is not reliable and you want to improve it.

After teaching courses in memory retention for a number of years, I have discovered that its study, far from being a matter of drudgery, can be made not only unexpectedly interesting but as entertaining as a parlour game. In fact, many of the exercises which are given in the following chapters have proved to be successful as parlour games. But while I want you to enjoy your work in improving your memory, you must not overlook the fact that work is necessary if you are to get any real benefit from the instruction given you.

Too many people have a tendency to complain of faulty memory without attempting to do anything to improve it, looking upon it as a handicap which must be borne and cannot be improved. And yet the rapid improvement in the memory after even a short effort is as startling as it is rewarding, and the importance of a good memory is beyond calculation.

What is the memory and how does it function? This morning, as you were drowsily shaking off the stupor of deep sleep, some sort of recollection rose immediately to the surface of your mind, a recent occurrence or some task to be performed during the day. In other words, at the very moment when your faculties became active, your memory began to function. To go a step further: *Every human activity rests in some way on memory*. It is logical to assume, therefore, that every piece of work can be accomplished more easily and more efficiently in direct proportion to the improvement in the functioning of the memory.

It isn't necessary to point out so obvious an example as the actor. His professional career depends almost entirely upon his memory and if that fails him he becomes unfit to perform.

To a lesser degree memory plays an important role in the life of the average business man. The merchant who can call to mind immediately his wholesalers, customers, buying and selling prices, personnel and so forth is more efficient than the one who is uncertain about these factors in his business life, who makes mistakes because he cannot remember figures or information accurately, who wastes his own time and that of others in prodding a faulty memory or hunting for information which he should have had on the tip of his tongue.

Let us imagine there are two salesmen, one 'of whom has a good memory, the other a poor one. The former immediately remembers the buyer's name when he meets him; he recalls his family connections and personal hobbies and, as a result, is able to discuss them and break down the difficult first few minutes of conversation and establish a personal contact with the buyer— an important result for the success of the business, as most good salesmen know. The man with the good memory has, of course, another advantage over the salesman with the poor memory. He is ready to give all the information that is required about his product without delay or hesitation, and he can keep in mind far more sales arguments than the untrained man.

Now let's see how memory affects the professional man—the lawyer, for example. If you are fortunate enough never to have been involved in a lawsuit, you must at least have followed criminal or civil trials in the newspapers. But have you observed how often the outcome of a trial was decisively influenced by the fact that one of the counsel could at the right moment refer the judge to a certain former ruling on a certain point of law? In such instances—in the midst of hearing the testimony of witnesses or the plea—there is no time to trundle out law books or commentaries, or to seek other decisions. The memory of the barrister must not fail him.

The late Max Steuer, once considered in America "the greatest trial lawyer of our time," was famous for his extraordinary memory. Richard O. Boyer narrates the following story in his biography of Steuer: "The factory of the Triangle Blouse Company had burnt down and the proprietors, who were defended by Steuer, were accused of causing the deaths of over a hundred of their girl employees by ordering that a certain exit be locked. One of the survivors, in the witness-box giving evidence for the prosecution, told a story that moved the crowded courtroom almost to a frenzy. The jurors wiped their eyes and scowled at the defendants, Steuer's clients. It appeared that a verdict of guilty was inevitable.

"As Steuer approached the girl to begin cross-examination, no one could have been more gentle or courteous. 'Now, Katie,' he said mildly, 'just tell your story again. Speak up so the jury can hear you.' Again the girl told her damaging story. Again the jury scowled at Steuer's clients. 'Katie, please tell your story again,' Steuer said, as she finished the second time.

" 'Katie, haven't you forgotten a word?' Steuer said

gently, as Katie completed her narration the third time.

"Katie studied a moment. 'Yes, sir, I forgot one word.'

" 'Well, tell the story again and put that word in it.'

"Katie obligingly did so. It was now apparent to the most slow-witted that Katie had learnt her story by heart. So Steuer transformed a dangerous witness into one whose testimony resulted in the acquittal of his clients."

But in order to win an acquittal, or in other words in order to notice the omission of a single word in a long narration, Steuer had to rely on his prodigious memory. Therefore we must acknowledge the importance of Boyer's statement, "Steuer has a freak memory, one which is as accurate as a typewritten transcript. He has an ear for phrases and sentences and can almost always recall them verbatim without recourse to the court record."

This is only one of thousands of cases in which the good memory of counsel not only influenced the verdict in a trial but actually decided it.

And what is said about the barrister holds true for the physician, too, especially for the surgeon, who has to act quickly and often with no time to prepare himself.

If he is to apply the correct treatment, he must remember not only the exact history of the case in question but also similar cases. If he himself has handled similar cases, he may encounter no difficulty, since our memories easily retain things which we have perceived with our own eyes or which are connected with our persons. But to remember his own cases is not enough; he must also remember cases described in medical literature. And that is a much more difficult task. In addition, he must be able to recognise his patients and to remember their names, although it is an established fact that most physicians have a rather poor memory for names and faces.

But apart from the importance of memory in one's professional and business life, it is of more immediate interest in its effect on our daily, personal life.

How many times a day do you rack your brain for the name of a person which "is just on the tip of your tongue," or find yourself in the embarrassing position of introducing your best friend and finding his name has slipped your mind? Or perhaps you had a number of errands to perform and discovered when you got home that you had forgotten the most important of them. The exasperation, the duplication of effort and the needless annoyance resulting from so poorly functioning a memory are familiar to all.

Equally familiar is the remark which would have dazzled the company and which you remember only after you are home and alone, too late to be of any use. And of more serious consequence is the telling argument which might decide favourably a business problem, or land you a job, or effect an important result, but which slips your mind at the time when you most need it.

A poor memory, as the foregoing illustrations will show you, is more than a mere annoyance. It is a serious handicap, but one which, with perseverance and intelligent effort, can be overcome.

Every advance in civilisation and every step in cultural progress rest in the last analysis upon memory. The Curies would never have discovered radium and the wonders of its potentialities if they had not kept in mind the radioactivity of all minerals containing uranium.

So every step forward in human achievement, every step forward of the individual as well as of humanity in general, depends upon memory. Our cultural heritage would be impossible if we could not recall what our fathers and forefathers thought, developed, and brought to fulfilment.

"People always talk about the weather," said Mark Twain, "but nobody does anything about it." And that is true too of the memory. You know that to maintain your health and general fitness for sports you must train your muscles, and consequently you go through your daily dozen or at least take extended walks to exercise your muscles and fill your lungs with oxygen. But you overlook entirely the fact that your memory is also a functioning part of you, and that it must be exercised and trained if it is to work in a satisfactory manner.

Of course, individuals differ widely in their inherent powers of memory, just as they do in other respects. But there are many instances that prove that even those least favoured by nature can, through zeal and effort, overtake the gifted. There is no real excuse, therefore, for accepting a poor memory as something which must be endured.

During my school-days I had a very bad memory. It was obvious to me that my classmates could retain facts longer and more accurately than I could, and for some time I accepted this as a natural and unchangeable situation, for young students are slow to learn that it is more important to retain facts in their mind than to continue to acquire further information which they aren't able to remember.

At the university I heard for the first time of courses in memory training and plunged into the subject with great enthusiasm.

In a short time I was able to train my memory to such a point that it has never since failed me! And yet the methods by which my memory was trained were faulty and rather crude. These faults I recognised more and more clearly later on in training my own classes, and during the course of many years and through the experience of working with thousands who have attended my lectures I have gradually eradicated them.

While this book on memory has been written with a view to making it as entertaining as possible, do not overlook the fact that the goal ahead is twofold: First of all, I want to give you keys to memory training which you can apply to any situation. Secondly, I want to improve your memory and, in time, strengthen it to such an extent that you will need to resort to the keys to memory training only in the rarest cases.

The attainment of this goal is a co-operative undertaking in which your part is indispensable—and that consists in more than merely reading the chapters of this volume; it requires actual study on your part. But you will be encouraged to discover that you do not need to wait until the end of the book to develop a better functioning of your memory. After a few chapters you will be able to undertake experiments in memory retention that would now seem utterly impossible to you.

When you have once made a beginning and learn not only that improvement in your memory is possible, but that it is actually taking place, you will find a new pleasure and new inspiration in your work. For my own part, I shall endeavour to explain each step clearly as I go along. This should enable you to grasp the basic principles and to make a successful application of them to your individual memory problems.

There are several points that should be made clear in the beginning:

1. Wherever mention is made of experiments, it is not sufficient for you to read about them; you must actually try them out in practice.

Only practice will bring you any practical benefit. Doing a thing is of infinitely more value than merely reading about it. Your muscles, for instance, are not developed or strengthened by looking at the pictures of physical exercises or reading how to perform them. Only by carrying out the exercises yourself will they do you any good.

The same is true with experiments in memory retention. Your powers of memory will not be improved by reading about these experiments and then forgetting them; only if you attempt to do them yourself, and practise them, will they be of any worth to you. But, in compensation for the effort you put into these exercises, you will find that your interest and pleasure in doing them will steadily increase.

2. A man who goes to a prize-fight must know the technique of boxing if he is to understand it. A man who wishes to improve his memory must know the technique that will develop it, a technique which we call *mnemonics*.

There are some rules for mnemonics which have been tried for several hundred years and found good, so that there is no reason for discarding them. Others serve special purposes and aims and their application depends on the requirements of the individual.

Take as an analogy an engineer who is commissioned to build a bridge over a river. If he does not want his entire structure to collapse, he must adhere to the basic and time-proven fundamental principles of construction. But he may choose his ornamental designs to suit his own tastes.

When these individual instances arise I will point out where it is advisable to make use of one set of rules and where to follow the other.

3. Do not make any experiments in mnemonics when

your brain is tired. While the human memory-capacity can be exercised and trained, the ability to absorb new facts has its limits, beyond which it is pointless to press. Whenever you begin to feel tired, interrupt your study and take a little rest.

If you have worked during the day to the point of exhaustion be sure to take at least an hour of complete rest before you begin your memory training. The fact that you are changing from one kind of work to another will be a great help. A complete change in mental activity is less wearing on the mind than extensive preoccupation in the same field.

4. Do not overlook the importance of diet in relation to brain work. The mind should not be greatly exerted on an empty stomach nor on one overloaded. When your stomach is empty, the brain refuses to function; on the other hand, the processes of digestion and cerebration are incompatible. Therefore, after a heavy meal it is essential to take a rest period.

5. The best time for study will vary according to your occupation and daily time-table. If you are busy all day with your work, you will naturally study at night. Otherwise, where time is at your disposal, there is no categorical answer as to the "best time." It depends entirely on your habits and inclinations.

Science has for some time acknowledged the fact that the mental receptivity of the individual at specific hours of the day differs as radically as the soundness of his sleep during various periods of slumber.

Some people fall into a deep, sound sleep in the early hours of the night, but sleep so lightly in the morning hours that they are awakened by the slightest noises. If you are one of these you are a morning worker, who can easily accomplish in the mornings work that would call forth great efforts at night.

The contrary, of course, holds equally true. People who find it difficult to fall asleep at night but sleep so heavily in the morning that they must be awakened by cold water are the evening or night workers. If you belong to this group you probably catch up in the evening, in intellectual pursuits, the time you idle away in the forenoon.

Up to a certain point it is possible to train one's natural inclinations by habit and discipline, but for this purpose it is unnecessary. Choose the hours which in your experience have proved to be most productive.

If you are parents of school children, this point is important in supervising their hours of study. It is often a mistake to force your son John to study his lessons at a particular time.

A knowledge of the psychological differences among individuals prevents many mistakes in disciplining children and also facilitates their learning processes.

6. Work as much as you can in the open air, instead of indoors, particularly if you must share a room with others. In working out some of the exercises which follow, it will help to be alone, or at least free from interruption. But whether you can be alone or not while you are studying, merely opening the window will be sufficient in providing fresh air so the brain may be stocked with new concepts and stirred to greater activity.

7. Repetition. The latest research findings in the domain of memory development have revealed that mere repetition in study is not so important as the time factor involved in the repetition. For instance, the research experiments of Professors Ebbinghaus, Duerr, Meumann, etc., have resulted in the following data:

The majority of experiments proved, as a general rule, that material which required 68 repetitions in one day could be mastered with only 38 repetitions if these were spread over three days. This proves, by the way, that the student who waits to the last day to "cram" would actually save half his time if he learned his subject gradually over a period of several days. The same is true for the adult. A subject which is hastily glanced over in one day can be retained for a longer period of time if a night is allowed to intervene before rereading.

The reason for this is that our memory, like all other functions of the consciousness, is not entirely inactive during the hours of sleep; it works on and on, in a more restricted sense, and for this reason impressions received on the previous day can impress themselves more deeply and register in the mind.

At some time or other you have probably worried desperately over some problem just before falling asleep, unable to find a solution. But on awakening the next morning, the solution was ready for you.

Folklore about the brownies who during the night do the work which was left uncompleted the preceding day is no doubt based on the experience of the race that this "dream work" is an actual fact.

One of the most interesting and credible examples of this dream work manifesting itself, not only intellectually but physically as well, is told by the well-known French writer, Mme. d'Espérance, in her book, *In the Kingdom of the Shadows*, which purports to be an autobiography.

She relates that when she was a schoolgirl she had to write, for homework, an essay on "What is Nature?" Writing essays was her weak point, and the task was particularly difficult for her. She postponed writing it from day to day until the evening before the day her composition was due. Still she could not write it. At last, she took her paper and pencil to bed with her and tried in despair to get on with her task. Finally, however, drowsiness overcame her and she fell asleep without having written a word.

In the morning she found, to her great surprise, many pages of written matter. The homework was not only complete but the composition was far beyond her usual ability in content and style. She would have believed that the brownies did it if she herself, as well as the teacher to whom she told the whole story, had not recognised the handwriting as undeniably her own.

The genuineness of the story we must leave to Mme. d'Espérance. But even though such a case is extremely rare, it is by no means unique. Such occurrences, moreover, furnish us with excellent proof of the matter in hand; namely, that the apperception, and with it the memory of mankind is not entirely obliterated during sleep.

And now we look forward to the goal we have set ourselves. Through the application of the method and exercises which have been developed for you, you will discover—apart from the actual improvement of your memory—that you have acquired an increased ability to concentrate so that distraction of attention will no longer disturb you.

You will be able, too, to overcome inhibitions which have prevented you from being a good speaker, and you will develop an increased ability to influence the actions and decisions of those about you as well as to overcome your own inferiority complex.

Here, then, if you are willing to give the following pages earnest study, is a road leading to increased achievement, with unexpected entertainment along the way, and a good memory as the goal.

CHAPTER II

THE RUDIMENTS OF MEMORY

EVERY outstanding man in the field of sports has a trainer, whether he be boxer, swimmer, or distance runner. Every day, however, you can see in sports arenas young men who attempt to compete without the advice of a trainer or a manager. The winner, they would probably tell you, is merely the man whose legs work the fastest, and that is all there is to it; apart from this, there is little to know about foot racing. But every adult knows that this is faulty reasoning.

Nurmi would never have been the runner par excellence without the help of good trainers. And why is this true? Because the trainer knows that racing is not merely a matter of putting one leg ahead of the other as fast as possible, but a matter of correct breathing, proper arm movement and posture, good pace and a dozen other details.

The trainer, in other words, has made a careful study of how the body functions *naturally* in running. He knows, consequently, in what respects it may fail to function and how such failure may be corrected.

To take another illustration: the invention of spectacles, opera glasses and the telescope was not possible until men had discovered how the human eye is constructed and how it functions in its natural state without the aid of glasses. Only with a complete understanding of the normal working of the eye would it be possible to correct vision, and remedy the defects which cause nearsightedness or far-sightedness. When one knows how the eye functions normally it is then possible, and only then, to grind glasses which will correct its shortcomings.

We know, then, that before we can make any improvement we must first know how the body or the particular organ under consideration operates in its natural, normal state. And this applies with equal force to the memory. Our first step must be to learn why we remember some things and forget others. No doubt, you have paid little attention to this uncertain quality of your memory but it will pay you to get to the root of it now.

Call to mind the last walk you took (it may be your walk to and from the office) yesterday or today. Please try to give definite answers to the following questions—and I would like to repeat here that only by attempting to answer the questions and practise the exercises which are given you can you expect this book to be of practical benefit to you.

1. Did you meet any acquaintances?
2. Can you describe the clothing worn by these acquaintances?
3. Did you talk to anyone during your walk?
4. Did you pass many shop windows?
5. Can you remember any displays shown in these windows?

Do not pass over these questions in a casual fashion, but answer them as definitely as you can. When you have done so, go over your answers a second time. You will doubtless wonder: Why have I remembered this and that and why have I forgotten the other? It is a well-known fact that we always remember a *part* of what we have seen and heard and forget the greater part.

This applies not only to the walk which we just tried

to remember but to our whole lives—starting in child-hood and school-days. But it is possible that you are wondering for the first time why this should be so.

All external impressions are received by the brain and registered in the brain cells. Why does our brain arbitrarily retain some of these while it forgets others after a shorter or longer time? To be sure, the passage of time plays a certain role, but it is not, obviously, the determining factor. The questions listed above, dealing with the very recent past (today or yesterday), prove this, as the short intervening time could not have affected your replies.

You may say that you have forgotten much that you saw in the walk because you only glanced at it once. But repetition of observation is not in itself a determining factor in remembering. If you would like to check this statement, ask an acquaintance what the 6 on his watch looks like, the watch which he consults many times daily. You will discover that most people, in spite of frequent observation, do not know whether their watches have Arabic or Roman numerals on the dial. A large number of them are unaware, until you call their attention to it, of the fact that the 6 is usually missing from watches, because the second hand takes its place.

We see, therefore, that neither the passage of time nor repeated observation can in itself explain the differences in "remembering" and "forgetting." The solution of the riddle is to be found in another phase of our minds.

Assume that we meet three friends who have just returned from a business trip together. One is a merchant, the second an architect, and the third a modiste. The three have visited a foreign city and have not parted company during the length of their stay. Therefore, the trio have seen the same sights and received the same impressions. Yet what happens when we ask each in turn to tell us what he saw?

The merchant will talk about the shops and stores he saw, and probably will describe window displays accurately, or store fixtures and furnishings.

The architect, on the other hand, will not refer to these things, but will devote a large part of his conversation to churches, monuments and public buildings. He will talk about Doric and Corinthian columns and give us an excellent description of this or that fine doorway.

The modiste, however, will overlook the things which attracted the merchant's attention and pass over the things discussed by the architect. Instead, she will describe in detail the costumes she saw in some café, and she might even be able to tell us about certain oddities in hats which she observed but fleetingly on passing strangers.

No doubt, you anticipated this difference in the impressions brought back by the three travellers because such cases are common to the experience of all of us. Yet this illustration has brought us much closer to the heart of our problem.

Each of the three travellers remembered the things which lay in his particular province, and we conclude, therefore, that human memory retains, from the countless impressions received during the day, only what touches on one's circle of interests. Whether one's interests are wide or restricted, whether they are great or petty, depends upon the individual and need not concern us. But the following conclusion is important:

As soon as a man's interest is aroused, he takes notice, that is, he turns his full attention to the object in question. This intensification of his attention we call concentration and we have discovered this principle: *Careful observation and concentration lay the foundation for good memory, and their application is easiest when the object of observation can be made interesting to the individual.*

Turn back to the five questions regarding your last walk. I think you will find that your answers are in accordance with the principle just stated.

For instance, you remember only the things of most interest to you in the conversation of your friends, don't you? You listened to these things with greater attention and concentration because they were of greater interest than the rest of the conversation, which you have now forgotten. In the same way, you will find that you remember some articles of clothing which your friends wear because they either especially please or displease you, but that you forget the rest.

To go back to your walk, you retained in your memory only those window displays from the hundreds you passed and looked at what particularly interested you, whether you were thinking of making a purchase or merely window shopping.

Through these illustrations and the simple test which you have just made of your own memory, you have discovered the most important principles on which the retention and forgetfulness of the human mind are based.

Now that we have seen how the normal memory functions, we are better able to correct the weaknesses which we find. We have a clearer idea of how to adjust the lever in order to lighten the load on our memories and to strengthen them so that they will function better both in quality and quantity of subject-matter. Our three objectives are:

1. To heighten our attentiveness and powers of observation.

2. To increase our ability to concentrate.

3. To draw hitherto unnoticed matters into the circle of our interest.

Rathenau once said the most difficult part of any task is to set a definite goal. But if one has a clear picture of his goal in mind, it is not too difficult to lay a straight course to it. Our three objectives are definitely set before us. Now we shall lay our course to reach them.

CHAPTER III

INDIVIDUAL METHODS OF OBSERVATION

ONE day the students in Privy Councillor Liszt's seminar in criminal law were startled when two students suddenly became embroiled in an argument which disrupted the sleepy quiet of the room, and rapidly developed into a violent quarrel, coming to blows. Before the horrified eyes of the students one of the two drew a revolver from his pocket and shot his opponent.

Abruptly Liszt turned to the students and asked them to write down an account of the incident. The encounter, of course, had been prearranged by Liszt and played in accordance with his instructions. Apart from the two participants, none of those present was aware that the scene was not spontaneous.

In spite of the fact that the whole incident had occurred before the very eyes of young men startled into keen attention, almost all of the accounts of the scene were incomplete or incorrect.

What Liszt wanted to prove through this experiment, and did prove, was the fact that most people have remarkably poor powers of observation. He had a second purpose in mind, as well, which was to point out that it is necessary to take extraordinary care in describing actual occurrences.

Day after day witnesses on oath testify to events which they have seen at first hand, describing them according to their best knowledge; and times without

29

number this testimony is false, because it rested on powers of observation which proved themselves, on cross-examination, to be unreliable.

It seldom happens that the faulty powers of observation in a witness are proved in the courtroom itself. But here is a case in point:

In several countries, for instance in France, it is possible to appeal against the verdict and carry a criminal case through the courts a second time with the same witnesses, etc., repeating the procedure of the first trial before a different judge.

In a criminal case of this sort, which was tried in the Court of Appeals, therefore for the second time, I was acting as counsel for the defence. The witness for the prosecution, on whose testimony the verdict was largely based in the first trial, had, according to her own assertions, caught but a hasty glimpse of the defendant at the scene of the crime, but she insisted emphatically that she could identify him. The accused categorically declared his innocence. The judge was inclined, like his predecessor in the first trial, to believe her sworn testimony.

When I asked her if her memory for faces was always so reliable that she could unfailingly depend upon it, she unhesitatingly answered in the affirmative. Now this witness had been the last to be interrogated in the second trial as well as in the first. Consequently the other witnesses in the case were already in the courtroom. But for several reasons, inconsequential to the present discussion, certain witnesses had been called in the second trial who had not been present at the first.

Immediately after the eye-witness in question had extolled her good memory for faces, I called on her to look at the witnesses in court and, relying on her allegedly good memory, to tell *which persons she had seen at the first trial and which she had not seen there*. The answer to my challenge was so calamitously wrong that even the prosecuting attorney could no longer deny the possibility of error on the part of the witness in recognising the defendant.

The case was dismissed, due to the fact that we had demonstrated *the faulty powers of observation* of a witness before the court, although this witness had so highly praised her good powers of observation. This incident will suffice as proof of man's weak apperceptive ability and his poor powers of observation.

Aristotle, one of the wisest men who ever lived, asserted that the common house-fly has four legs! This in itself would not be of much importance, but the statement was repeated in textbook after textbook up to the middle of the last century, in spite of the fact that it is really not difficult to see and prove that the common house-fly has six legs.

But it is not enough merely to confirm the fact that powers of observation are faulty. It is more to the point to find ways and means of correcting them. In order to do this, we must recognise the importance of the *five senses*. On them depend our powers of perception. Our memories can retain only those impressions which have been made on our minds through the senses of sight, hearing, smell, taste or feeling. Of these five senses, *sight and hearing* play immeasurably greater roles than the other three.

The difference between the various brands of cigarettes or vintages of wine lies solely in *taste*. If we did not retain a memory of their special flavours, it would be impossible for us to make a distinction between the various brands, and the cigarette manufacturers as well as the wine merchants might as well stop advertising specific brands.

It is *sight and hearing*, however, which play the most important part in daily life. Let us look at these two senses for a moment in order to determine which of the two is the more important.

No doubt you have personal acquaintances who, years after they have left school, can still remember exactly where in their schoolbooks a certain passage is located. By that I mean that they can distinctly remember that the Battle of Waterloo is at the bottom of a left-hand page, while the Fall of Rome is about in the middle of a right-hand page. These same people usually remember very little of the lectures they attended unless they took down copious notes.

When studying a foreign language they do not learn much from hearing the words spoken; they need to write down the words themselves or at least to see them written or printed. These people depend upon eye impressions. They are the visual, or eye-minded type.

In contradistinction to them are those people who retain the gist of a lecture they have heard far better than the substance of a book they have read. Years later they can recall the very words used by their teacher or professor on a given topic, long after the impression of the printed page has vanished.

When these people call absent friends or acquaintances to mind, it is the timbre of their voices rather than their outward appearance that they clearly and reliably recall. We call these people, whose memory is based on hearing, the acoustical, or ear-minded type.

Great musicians obviously belong to this type, while great painters, of course, belong to the eye-minded type.

Modern psychology recognises a third type besides these two basic types—the motor-minded. But it is sufficient for our purposes to restate the fact that schools and colleges have failed in training both of the basic types. If we were logical and sensible we would classify all secondary-school pupils, or at least all college students, according to their types of memory, and urge them to plan their courses of study accordingly.

Of what value is a true knowledge of and differentiation between the eye-minded and the ear-minded types? The answer is: The acutely ear-minded student cannot do better than choose lecture courses, since what he hears makes the deepest impression on his memory. Furthermore, he should not take too many notes but confine himself to cue words. Attending lectures is without doubt more beneficial for him, as well as more time-saving, than studying from a book.

The opposite, of course, holds true for the eye-minded. By reading, he can master his lessons in a fraction of the time that his attendance at lectures would consume. These are elementary matters that would result in a great reduction of time for the entire course of study, and up to now far too little attention has been paid to them.

To what type do you belong? It must be understood that no one is 100 per cent ear-minded or 100 per cent eye-minded. Nevertheless, either one or the other type of memory is sufficiently predominant in the individual to classify him definitely.

If, after reading the foregoing paragraphs, you are undecided about the type to which you belong, or you wish to classify your friends or children, try the following test:

Write down ten different words and then read them aloud to the person you are testing. He is to write down a different word suggested by each word you dictate. He should not make any special effort but should merely write down the first word that comes into his head after hearing your word dictated.

Now take his list of words and compare them with your list, which you read aloud to him. You will find that the eye-minded person has written down words that resemble yours visually, while the ear-minded person has written down words that have a tonal relationship with yours.

For instance, if you have read "wall," the eye-minded person writes down such words as picture, room, curtain, door, etc. But the ear-minded person writes ball, call, mall, or the like.

If you have read "sun," the eye-minded individual writes heavens, moon, stars, light, etc.; the ear-minded run, fun, ton, etc.

Naturally, in a book on memory training it is not sufficient merely to determine the type to which we belong; it is essential to attempt at once to effect an improvement.

As a matter of fact, all the senses of man can be developed with relatively little effort. You will discover this for yourself in regard to the powers of observation, if you will practise the exercises which I have arranged for you. But remember that you must practise these exercises faithfully and not merely read about them.

EXERCISES IN SIGHT TRAINING

1. Take from 6 to 10 sheets of paper of the same size. On the first sheet draw 6 parallel, perpendicular lines of equal length. On the second sheet draw 7; on the third 8, etc., always adding one line to the new sheet. Be sure, however, to keep the same amount of margins between the first and last lines and the edges of the paper on each sheet, so that the total area of parallel lines takes up the

same amount of space, regardless of their number.

Then shuffle the sheets in a heap and take out one sheet after the other at random. At a glance tell how many lines are on each sheet. The errors that always are made in the beginning soon disappear with practice. But the point of the experiment is to do this exercise as quickly as possible and to recognise the number at a swift glance at the sheet.

2. After you have practised this exercise for a time you can extend it to the point where you can tell at a glance the number of windows in a house you have passed on your walk; or correctly estimate, at sight, the number of books in a strange library; or decide the size of an audience at a lecture by a quick survey of the hall.

Of course, it is always necessary to choose only such experiments as can be checked for accuracy; for instance, the library of an acquaintance who knows exactly how many books he has, or who would willingly count them to prove your estimate.

3. Another exercise for training the eye, which, however, calls for considerably more effort, is the following: Hunt up a shop window that has a good many items on display (not furniture, for the window would have room for only a few pieces). A window that has price tags on the articles is preferable. Look at the window display closely and carefully and take special note of any singularities.

Then leave the window and find a quiet spot in the neighbourhood and write down everything you saw in the window, sketching it if you can. If the individual articles had price tags on them, you should include them.

Return to the window with your sheet of paper and compare what you have written with the actual articles, but do not correct what you have written during this comparison before the display. Rather, impress your errors on your mind and then make your corrections on your sheet in the spot you originally found at a distance from the window. Then go back and compare your list with the window again and, if necessary, correct it again as before. Do not be content until your list is correct in every detail.

Test yourself frequently in this way, with many different window displays, and you will soon have the satisfaction of finding that your mistakes in memory grow fewer and of less importance.

If you find it too difficult at first to remember the contents of a window display, start with attempting to remember in detail the furnishings of a room.

There is a still simpler form of this exercise—a game which is excellent for developing quick powers of observation in children. Take ten or twelve small objects, such as a watch, pencil, purse, eraser, etc. Place these articles on a table and let the children look at them for a short while.

Promise a small prize to the child who can tell or write down the largest number of objects he has viewed. Such a game spurs the children to competition, since they are naturally competitive, and try to surpass one another in order to win the prize. At the same time their powers of observation are being stimulated. But be sure to gauge the number and complexity of articles with respect to the age of the children.

4. The following experiment is useful for training yourself in quick observation: Draw a square enclosing 25 smaller squares, like a chessboard. In each square put down one of the numbers 1 to 25, or letters of the alphabet—but arrange them haphazardly, *not in sequence*. Do not look at this chessboard for a day or two.

Then sit down to it again and number or letter the

squares in their proper order. This exercise in itself presents no difficulties; it is a question of ease and celerity. Therefore it is important for you to keep score of how many seconds it has taken you the first, second, third and succeeding times you have tried it.

You can make the experiment more complex by numbering the chess squares with multiple digits or with two letters of the alphabet, or with a capital and a lower-case letter. Although such divergence in letters does not change it, it makes the game more difficult because it confuses the eye of the player.

EXERCISES IN HEARING

1. Seated at home or in your office, countless small noises reach your ears. Some of them are house noises heard through the walls or ceiling; others, street noises. Try to distinguish between these various sounds and be sure of what you heard in each instance. You must, of course, pay attention to details. It is not enough to know that you heard footsteps outside your door. From the sound and manner of the tread try to determine whose step it was.

2. Now go out in the street. The sounds which the ear catches are more numerous, more irregular; and above all, less familiar. As many sounds are heard at the same time it is not easy for the beginner to differentiate between them. But even here repeated practice will bring quick results.

While it is wise, in the beginning, to choose unfrequented streets for this exercise, after a little while you will be able to go into busier thoroughfares, then to work your way into the centre of town and into the thick of noises.

A similar exercise may be practised in the country, in

the woods or fields. Here, too, there are constant small noises, the only difference being that here they are made by birds and small animals, instead of by buses, and other noisy vehicles.

The small sounds heard in the open are familiar to the man who lives in the country, but the city man will have to orient himself a bit at the zoo or an aviary before he can tell one sound from another.

For this reason, however, it is wise for the city man and farmer alike not to confine their exercises to their own communities. Try to alternate between city and country so that you will be able to distinguish between these completely different kinds of noise.

Practise these exercises in eye and ear training faithfully for a while and you will notice a great improvement in your powers of observation. Things you previously overlooked or forgot you will observe clearly and remember.

Here is a rather amusing problem, the solution of which rests entirely on close attention to wording. Try to solve it for yourself before you read the correct solution. Later you may wish to try it on your friends:

Two volumes of a book are standing in correct order next to each other on a library shelf. Each volume is 3 inches thick, including front and back cover, which are each $\frac{1}{8}$ inch thick. A bookworm eats its way from Page 1, Volume I, to the last page of Volume II. How far has it travelled?

I have often used this problem in my classes and invariably get the answer $5\frac{3}{4}$ inches. This of course is wrong. To solve it correctly, you must visualise the two volumes. They are standing in their correct order on the shelf. If you cannot visualise them, go to a bookcase and look at any two-volume book. You will see at once that

Page 1 of Volume I and the last page of Volume II are on the inside; that is, the two pages are separated only by the front cover of Volume I and the back cover of Volume II. The correct answer, therefore, is $\frac{1}{8}$ inch plus $\frac{1}{8}$ inch, or $\frac{1}{4}$ inch.

If you put this question, simple as it is, to a circle of friends, you will find out how few people can visualise the simplest matter, for instance, the relative positions of the two volumes of a book.

Many leaders of industry are convinced that efficiency in their employees is often determined by their powers of observation.

A furniture manufacturer who attended my lectures told me one day that it was his practice to give all applicants for positions tests in observation and perception. After asking the usual questions about training, experience and references, he tried the applicants out in some actual situation. For instance, if a load of timber had just been delivered in the yard, he sent the applicant down to find out about it and report on it. If the latter returned with no further information than that the timber was being delivered, he was considered unsuited to the job and sent away. The report which the applicant was expected to make ran somewhat as follows:

The delivery which is being unloaded is walnut from the Blank Company in C—, for which you placed an order. It is exceptionally fine wood. About two thirds of the delivery is unloaded and it will take an hour more to complete the job. The yard foreman is supervising the unloading. He gave orders to store the wood in Warehouse 3.

A report of this sort is comprehensive. It shows that the applicant was a close observer, and was resourceful in asking pertinent questions about points which did not come under his own observation.

This manufacturer declared emphatically—and I affirm it from personal experience—that a man's powers of observation are almost always indicative of his producing capacities.

CHAPTER IV

HOW TO REMEMBER PLACES, COLOURS AND FORMS

Up to this point we have studied only the functioning of the memory. Now let us turn to the various objects which we wish to remember.

When you are in a circle of intimate friends, turn the conversation on the subject of memory. You will be amazed at the conclusions drawn by the various individuals about their own memories.

One of them has no difficulty in recalling numbers, names and dates, but confesses he can never remember persons no matter how often he has seen or spoken to them. The next always remembers faces but can never recall names. One of those present—usually a man— says that he never loses his way in a neighbourhood where he has once set foot, but that he cannot describe the architecture of a single building in it.

A woman, on the other hand, complains that she has no sense of direction and that she confuses the points of the compass. She even finds it difficult not to lose her way in localities which are quite familiar to her. And yet she can give her dressmaker a detailed description of a model of which she has had only a passing glimpse in a shop window.

Apart from these examples, you know from your own experience how variously the individual memory functions in learning a foreign language or in recalling melodies.

From the foregoing we may conclude that it is a mistake for people to speak in generalities about a "good" memory or a "poor" memory. The human memory is never completely good or completely poor. It is good or poor only in reference to particular material, and we must, therefore, make distinctions between a memory for faces, names, numbers, facts, and a memory for tunes, foreign languages, etc.

With this fact in mind, we come to the methods for improving the memory in each of these particular fields, for obviously the great differences in the cases call for wide differences in method.

For the present we will defer a discussion of numbers, faces, names, dates and facts, because they can be dealt with more satisfactorily with the help of mnemotechnical aids, which will be considered in a later chapter. But a faulty memory for places, forms and colours can be corrected in a natural, simple way, and the method which I propose will bring results in a short while.

HAVE YOU A GOOD MEMORY FOR PLACES?

Can you find your way in a strange city with the help of a map, or retrace your steps over a particular route which you have been over only once? If you cannot, I recommend this method.

If you live in a large city, go to some part of it into which you seldom if ever venture. If you live in a small town or in the country, you can practise this exercise with best results when you are making a trip or go to another town.

In any case, select a route, preferably irregular and circuitous, which will take you some twenty or thirty minutes to walk. As you go along, pay particular attention to landmarks, especially those on corners where you turn to right or to left. For instance, notice any striking house fronts, monuments, shop windows, and the like. When you reach the end of your walk, try to recall every detail that you noticed on the way and retrace your steps in memory. If you can do so, make a little sketch showing the important landmarks on the way.

Then try to retrace your steps in the opposite direction, mentally of course, using your landmarks as guides. If you cannot find your way back to your starting point, in spite of your memorised landmarks, repeat the exercise again and again until you know the way perfectly.

This exercise in orientation may seem difficult to you at first, but if you try it often, in different localities, you will ultimately succeed. Your eye and brain gradually accustom themselves to watching automatically for landmarks. After you have mastered this exercise you will find that even in a strange city you will not lose your sense of direction when following a route on a map. Your practised and sharpened sense of direction will not fail you, no matter how long a route you choose.

HAVE YOU A GOOD MEMORY FOR GEOGRAPHY?

Without consulting an atlas, sketch a rough outline map of England, Wales and Scotland. Remember that unless you actually work out these exercises this book cannot be of real assistance to you. While it is not necessary for your sketch to show odd conformations of the land, it should be a reasonably correct outline. When you have completed the rough outline, put in the following, in the order given:

London
Edinburgh
Cornwall

The boundary between England and Scotland
The boundary between England and Wales
The Caledonian Canal
Manchester
Cardiff
The River Thames
The Pennines

When you have completed your map, compare it with an atlas to check your memory for geography. Find out to what extent it has failed you.

Now make a rough sketch of Ireland, again without referring to an atlas. Show the boundary between Northern Ireland and Eire and the positions of Belfast and Dublin. Then compare your map with the atlas and correct your mistakes.

If these exercises are too difficult, start by making sketches of sections of the country with which you are familiar, which you have visited and know from your own experience.

Remember that the important thing about these exercises is not meticulous accuracy, but the ability to outline from memory, without reference to an atlas.

I can still remember my geography lessons in school. At that time map drawing was often set for homework and the best mark was given to the pupil whose map looked most like the one in the atlas, with the ocean coloured an attractive blue and the mountains a pretty brown.

My teacher, like many of his colleagues, had not the faintest knowledge of the psychology of memory. He did not know that a rough sketch done from memory and later compared with the atlas was of far greater value in impressing the outlines of a foreign country than the handsomest map copied, or even traced, from a book.

Don't make the same mistake in your study of geography or in teaching the subject to your children! The correct way to memorise the shape of a foreign country, its rivers, lakes, mountains, and cities is as follows:

1. Make a sketch map of the country from memory.

2. Compare your rough draft with the atlas and correct your mistakes.

3. Lay this map aside and make a new one, again from memory.

4. Compare it with the atlas and again correct your errors.

5. When this second (or third, or fourth, if need be) map meets with your approval, wait several days and then make a new one from memory.

If you do this exercise often enough, you will notice a great improvement in your memory for geography. You will find yourself, in time, able to conjure up the appearance of any country or city when you hear its name spoken or see it in print, and you will take a more intelligent interest in geographical names when you encounter them.

HAVE YOU A GOOD MEMORY FOR COLOURS?

Go to a picture gallery, look at any painting, and then, at home or in another part of the gallery, try to visualise all the details and colours of the picture. Again a rough sketch will be of aid to you.

You need not have any artistic talent whatsoever to do this exercise. It isn't necessary to make a beautiful sketch. The essential thing is to discover how much your memory has retained of the details and, above all, of the colours of the painting which you selected.

Now, go back for another view of the painting, compare your sketch with the original, correct your mistakes, and repeat the process until your visualisation and memory of colour and details are absolutely correct.

You will doubtless meet with difficulties the first time you try this exercise. But it will encourage you to find that these difficulties will gradually disappear with practice and that your memory for colours, forms, and the like grows.

The following story serves to illustrate how a practised and trained memory functions in this capacity:

One of the most beautiful and valuable paintings in St. Peter's Church in Cologne was the Rubens altarpiece. It depicts the martyrdom of one of the apostles. In 1805 a French soldier stole the picture as a war trophy and took it to France. As the painting had been a great favourite, the people of Cologne were reluctant to hang a different picture in its place. Thereupon a painter in the city offered to make a copy of it *from memory*, and the copy was hung in place of the original.

Many years later the original was returned by the French and the remarkable fact was discovered that the copy was so like the original, even in the smallest details, that one could hardly differentiate between them. Had the painter made his copy directly from the original he would have been considered merely a good copyist and the story would hold little interest. But he made it entirely from memory, after the original had been removed, and the incident serves as proof of what a trained memory for colour and form can accomplish.

Have You a Good Memory for Architectural Detail?

Make a rough sketch of your own house front from memory, without going out to look at it. From memory sketch any striking building, such as a church or library, which you frequently pass.

Compare your sketches with the originals, correct your mistakes, and continue with the method outlined above for improving your memory of geography.

By this time you have enough examples so that you can continue independently with the development of memory for objects which are not dealt with here. Bear in mind, however, that so far we have considered only such simple subjects in memory training as can be mastered without the aid of mnemonics.

For more difficult subjects—numbers, names, dates, etc.—mnemotechnical aids are indispensable, and later on we shall see how even the most difficult things can be memorised and retained through mnemonics.

CHAPTER V

THE DEVELOPMENT OF CONCENTRATION

THE *memory has no enemy greater than lack of concentration.* To go back to the story of the three travellers who made a trip together and then told what they had seen on their journey, it is apparent that the things they recalled were those on which they had concentrated their attention.

From the preceding chapters you have learned also that the ability to concentrate is important in every effort of memory. For instance, if, while you are reading a book on travel in Britain, you begin to think of holidays you have spent on the Continent, you will remember little of what you read.

Unfortunately, the present-day emphasis on political crises, threats of war and sensational news is an enemy of concentration. It tends to develop nervousness and lack of concentration.

The more taut the nerves become in the struggle for daily bread, security, even preservation of one's self and family, the more difficult it is to shake off the cares of daily life and concentrate on a certain subject.

The term "concentration" has become rather hackneyed through constant loose usage, and it has a more exact meaning than is commonly given it.

Many people believe they are "concentrating" to a sufficient degree when they succeed in doing their jobs competently even when surrounded by distracting noises. That this is not true concentration is evident when one attempts any sort of reasonably simple experiment demanding real, authentic concentration.

Europeans, we must confess, are greatly inferior in the art of concentration to Asiatics, especially Hindus. For hundreds of years Indian fakirs and yogis have practised concentration systematically, and they have passed their art along from generation to generation.

At this point I should like to cite as examples two stories from the countless numbers told by returning travellers. These stories are believed credible by so many people that we cannot doubt their authenticity.

The first is the so-called Magic Mango Tree:

For this performance the yogi lets the bystanders approach as closely as they please while he heaps a little mound of sand together before their eyes. Into this sand he puts a little seed which he has brought with him and covers the whole with a cloth. He then seats himself in the characteristic yogi pose and slowly waves his hand back and forth over the covered mound.

After a short while the cloth begins to rise under the very eyes of the spectators and they see that the cloth is being lifted by a plant forcing its way up through the sand. As the cloth continues to rise, the yogi keeps up the monotonous waving of his hands and the plant grows to giant proportions. Soon the astonished spectators see an Indian mango tree whose size is described variously by the different observers, all of whom, nevertheless, agree that it towers over the person of the yogi.

The remarkable fact is that the tourists to India unanimously declare that the tree grew in so lifelike a manner before their eyes that no one could doubt its actual existence. And yet this audience was composed of tourists who had heard of the experiment long before they saw it and who knew that in reality there was no tree at all, merely an optical illusion. In spite of this knowledge, however, the yogi's power of concentration could conjure up this "suggestion."

All sorts of attempts have been made to explain this phenomenon, but in vain. One theory, for instance, is that the yogi conceals somewhere about him little India-rubber plants of varying sizes. These unusual plants can, as a matter of fact, be pressed into so small a ball that they are scarcely larger than an egg.

When a conjurer on the stage imitates this experiment, he hides little rubber plants of varying sizes under the cloth and produces them one after the other before the eyes of the spectators by clever manipulation.

Other conjurers use little mango trees whose branches have been hollowed out, rather like wood canals. In these canals they place young locusts and tie their hind legs to the branches with fibres of bast.

When the conjurer sprinkles a fine powder into the canals, the locusts come out of hiding, but, because they are tied, they remain sitting on the little branches. As the wings of these locusts are deceptively similar to leaves, the little tree seems to the spectators to be rich in foliage.

These attempts to explain the phenomenon are useless, however, when the performer has no opportunity to conceal anything. They become pointless when one sees a photograph taken by one of the spectators. The incorruptible photographic plate shows no trace of a real tree in spite of the fact that the spectators were convinced and swore under oath that they had actually seen a tree.

This difference between what the human eye believes to be true and what the plate discloses proves the experiment to be true hallucination.

Later on we shall discuss the origins of such hallucinations. In the present connection it is sufficient to confirm the fact that extraordinary powers of concentration on the part of the yogi are necessary in performing the feat, for he is rarely in a position to bolster his experiment with explanations, since his spectators from overseas understand his language as little as he understands theirs.

Another experiment calling for similar powers of concentration, also reported by many tourists in India, is *imperviousness to pain.*

Indian fakirs and yogis have the faculty of concentrating so firmly on the idea of absence of pain that they are able to pierce their tongues, cheeks and the muscles of their upper arms with long needles. At times they leave the needles in place for more than ten minutes and actually are unaware of pain, conducting the experiment with a quiet smile.

We may rest assured that we shall never attain the yogi's remarkable power of concentration, since he has two advantages over us: his inheritance from past generations and the strict attention paid to the subject throughout his schooling.

But, on the other hand, we can without doubt increase our power of concentration to a very high degree and at the same time conduct a successful fight against absent-mindedness.

As exercises in concentration I recommend the following:

1. Stretch out in a comfortable position on a couch or bed and be careful to relax your whole body, with no strain or tension anywhere.

Close your eyes and try to *visualise the form* of some simple, familiar article. As soon as you succeed in doing so, concentrate your thoughts on this article to the exclusion of everything else and do not let them stray in any direction if you can help it.

Suppose, for example, you choose an electric light bulb. You must keep your mind on the bulb and not let it stray to the chandelier or the room it illuminates or the people in the room.

At first it will be difficult for you to sustain this experiment for longer than four or five seconds. But by gradual, regular drill, you will succeed in running the time of concentration up to ten seconds or longer.

When you have learned to do this, make the experiment more difficult. Instead of the quiet room, select a more or less populous spot where you are unable to stretch out in a position conducive to concentration, and where, moreover, the impressions on eye and ear will make it more difficult for you to collect your thoughts.

2. A more difficult, and consequently more interesting, exercise in concentration consists in remembering as exactly as possible the occurrences of the hour immediately preceding this. It is not sufficient for you to recall only that you bought an evening paper or had a whisky and soda. The correct method of carrying out the experiment would be somewhat as follows:

"It is now six o'clock. At five I left my office in ————— Street and went to ————— Underground Station. On the way there the window of X's shop caught my eye because it contained a particularly good-looking suit. I stood in front of the window and wondered whether my income and my expenses for the current month would let me buy a new suit. The answer was No, because I had a rather large bill for electricity this quarter. But I noted the name of the tailor and decided that I could afford a suit next month.

"I entered the Underground Station, bought my ticket at the booking office where I got some change, went down the moving staircase and waited several minutes for my train. During this time I thought about this matter and that which had kept me busy all afternoon and about which I had not yet reached a decision. In the Underground train I noticed two people sitting near me. One was a man who was sitting across from me. I noticed him because he wore a peculiar-looking tie. The other was a woman who resembled a relative of mine. During my journey I thought about a problem or two which worried me. . . ."

If you carry out the exercise in this manner, you will make an important experiment in concentration: the more detailed, the better. That is, the more particulars you can recall, the more value the exercise will have for you. Of course, it is impossible for you to remember all the people you saw on the Underground or all the thoughts that passed through your mind during the journey. But you will find that diligent, patient practice will increase your abilities.

It is important to remember that, apart from increasing your ability to concentrate, this exercise will in time make it possible for you to remember with a considerable degree of accuracy conversations which you have held and sensations which you have experienced. It is hardly necessary to point out how useful this can be in daily life.

And, finally, here is a third exercise which should appeal particularly to those of you who have lively imaginations:

Everyone occasionally falls into day-dreaming. There can be no objection to that, provided these day-dreams do not interfere with more serious thinking. You can turn them into an interesting exercise in concentration if you make an attempt to recall your whole train of thought as exactly as possible. For example:

Mr. X is sitting on the beach in summer, enjoying the breeze. He sees a passing sailing-boat. It reminds him of the little sailing-boat his son received a few days before as a present from an aunt. He remembers he must buy another postcard for the aunt, and that he has just seen some especially attractive cards in a shop window. This reminds him that a road map was lying next to the cards with enticing tours in the neighbourhood traced on it, and he muses that it really was too bad he had left his car at home because he could have made such pleasant trips in it.

Suppose that at this point Mr. X decided to do the above-mentioned exercise in concentration. He would try, starting with his car, to trace his entire train of thought backwards. That is, from the car to the road map, the postcards, the aunt, his little boy and the toy sailing-boat, to the actual sailing-boat which started him off on his train of thought.

Since reveries are apt to be rather long drawn out, tracing them backwards is often—especially at the beginning—quite difficult. But if a person practises it often enough he will make excellent headway and with very little effort not only strengthen his ability to concentrate, but his memory as well.

Why do so many people neglect their powers of concentration or make so little effort to improve them? The real explanation, probably, is that concentration is an abstract idea whose practice does not always show concrete results.

For instance, if you are studying an instrument such as the violin, you notice after a few practice periods that your tone and phrasing improve. If you are studying a foreign language, you notice after a little while that you can read books in this language or even converse with others in it. But in studying concentration, no such immediate, noticeable results are evident. Its benefits are only indirectly evident in a greater ease of learning, greater capacity of remembering and greater control over your environment. But these are all things which cannot be measured by rule or weighed in a scale.

And yet the ability to concentrate is no less important. We shall return to it again and again and you will discover that it is indispensable to the memory and to suggestion.

But in the meantime let us consider the third essential factor in the efficient functioning of the memory—association of ideas.

CHAPTER VI

ASSOCIATION OF IDEAS

A SHORT time ago I read that English is spoken by about 260 million people in the world. As I was reading, I had a telephone call from Mr. Dayton whom I hadn't heard from for a long time. He gave his address as 365 West Street and the postal number of the district in which he lived as 7.

Let us consider these two items from the viewpoint of memory. How can I remember them? I am quite sure that I shall *not* remember them without some form of association. The number of people who speak English, an astronomical number, is difficult to keep in mind. But if I ponder the number for a little while, I realise that there are 26 letters in the English alphabet; and then it is easy for me to think of ten million people to each letter.

When I think about my phone caller's address, I notice that the house number corresponds to the days in a year and the postal district number to the days in a week. Having noticed this coincidence, I am very sure I shall never forget the address, even though the person's name is not *Day* or *Weeks* or *Year*sley.

Of course, associations are not always so easy or so obvious as in these two selected cases. Let us examine our facts:

In the case of the English-speaking people, the

number 260 million was new and had to be remembered. The number 26 was well known as the number of letters in the alphabet and therefore convenient to serve as a hook for the number which was to be kept in mind.

In the case of the phone caller, the numbers 365 and 7 were new and had to be remembered. However, both figures were familiar in another connection and therefore suitable for serving as a hook for the address which I intended to keep in mind. So we may draw this conclusion: Whether a connection is obvious or not, the fact remains that *the new always imposes itself on our minds through association with something already known.*

This statement applies to the entire work of memory. For example, consider just how you learn a foreign language. If you wish to learn that horse is *equus* in Latin, you have no recourse but to associate this hitherto unfamiliar word *equus* with the familiar concept horse. And it makes no difference whether you learn the word from a book or hear it spoken in conversation (in the latter case, with a Latin word, this is not apt to happen). *The necessity for associating the word with the familiar concept* horse *remains the same.*

You can observe this principle at work in every child who is learning to talk. The child is acquainted with the idea of doll long before he knows the name of it. Then when he hears the name *doll* he associates it with the familiar concept of his toy. It is for this reason that one must be so careful before children in the use of words.

Suppose you have a fox terrier. If you refer, before the child, to this pet as "fox terrier" instead of "dog" the child will form the wrong concept. That is, he will apply the words fox terrier to all dogs that he sees, no matter what breed they are. Lack of attention to this matter will account for the fact that children so often have to unlearn what they have learned. That is, the child must form a generic notion of dog and then learn that fox terriers are only a certain breed of dog.

The work of memory in the child is in this respect similar to the work of memory in the adult, and we always find this rule holding true: *When a man learns anything new, no matter what the subject-matter, it is always learned and remembered through association with familiar knowledge.*

But this confirmation of fact does not help us much. We must look further and try to classify our thoughts about the ways in which this association and relationship function. We cannot avoid this difficult task if we are to learn not merely how the memory works but how we can improve the functioning of our memories.

Returning to the items given above, I can obviously proceed in two different ways: I can visualise the letters of the alphabet, picturing each being spoken aloud by ten million people in chorus; and I can *visualise* Mr. Dayton with a calendar under his arm, reminding me of the connection with his person and the divisions of the year and week.

On the other hand, I can *reason*, without forming a mental picture, that the English alphabet consists of twenty-six letters and that I must multiply this number by ten million. I can also reason, without the mental image of a calendar, that there are 365 days in a year and seven in a week, and I can form a logical connection between these facts and Mr. Dayton.

From these associational possibilities we establish this statement: *Whenever we undertake to learn something new, we can either associate it visually with familiar facts or relate it logically through pure reason.*

Of these two possibilities in association of ideas, the visual is by far the stronger, for most human beings remember events and other matters better when they have seen them happen before their very eyes than when they merely hear or read about them. That is why, in the study of physics, the pupils are called upon to make experiments themselves, because the teacher knows that *experiments seen make a deeper impression than experiments read.*

If you have taken pictures while on holiday, the entire holiday comes to life again through a perusal of your pictures. It makes no difference whether you have taken snapshots of the countryside or of persons. In either case the pictures themselves quickly and clearly call to mind the impressions of your journey. Every advertiser knows that a good advertisement calls for a picture. The psychological reason is always the same:

The pictorial always makes the best impression and a deep impression is always the aim and purpose of the advertiser.

If you want to bring home to your mind the boundary line between England and Scotland, a mental picture of the map is of far greater aid to the memory than an oral description which says that the boundary begins a little south of Gretna Green, goes up Liddesdale, follows the line of the Cheviot Hills, then cuts off north to the Tweed and ends a little way north of Berwick-upon-Tweed.

And finally, the simplest of examples: If you have ever seen Nelson's Column or the Eiffel Tower, your memory will retain a clearer and surer picture of it than if you had read a whole array of descriptions of these two monumental structures.

Because pictorial impressions are the strongest, it is apparent that in memorising and in remembering, in all that the memory retains, it is essential to make visual associations.

I should like to give you some examples of what I call visual associations:

Suppose we take the words "cat" and "fence." Since we are accustomed to seeing cats on a back fence, it is easy to imagine a cat running along a fence.

If you take the words "flowers" and "lamp," there is no natural connection between the two, but it is not too difficult to imagine a lamp decorated with a flower design or that flowers are standing on a table lighted by a lamp. But if we take the words "chess-board" and "thrush," we must have a lively imagination to form a suitable mental image of them. Perhaps the chess-board is laid out in a garden over which a thrush is flying. Such mental images may often seem far-fetched. But a few such exercises convince one that it is precisely such unreal images that make deep impressions and are easily remembered because of their absurdity or oddity.

Notice that all these illustrations deal with the association of concrete objects. In other words, we have heretofore restricted ourselves to things we can see with our own eyes. This task becomes considerably more difficult when we undertake abstract ideas, that is, those that cannot be apprehended visually. No matter how good your imagination, you cannot form a mental picture of the words "virtue" and "pride." If you attempt a mental picture of the two, you are restricted to substituting concrete images for the abstract.

For instance, you may think of an angel instead of virtue, and teacher's pet instead of pride. But for your peace of mind, let me assure you that the necessity for forming abstract concepts rarely occurs in everyday life, except in listening to lectures or speeches. So we need not pay much attention or give much time to these exceptions.

Let us rather return to our investigation of concrete visual ideas. From the examples just quoted you can easily see that visual association implies imagination.

And here is something to think about.

As much as I have lectured on this subject and as many classes as I have taught in it, I have seldom met anyone who does not insist that he has an excellent imagination. In answer to the question: "Do you have a good imagination? Can you visualise things that really do not exist?" almost everyone says "Yes." As the imaginative powers of individuals vary greatly, such unanimity of opinion is rather startling. I think the reason for it is that there is scarcely a human characteristic so difficult of comparison as imagination.

Whether you are quicker at figures than your friend X is easy to determine, if you both add identical columns of figures. Whether you or your friend Y can speak French better is readily determined by a joint reading of a French newspaper or a conversation with a Frenchman.

In short, almost all of a man's characteristics and abilities can be compared with those of another man. One could always run a contest in them to determine them, as has been done in the case of shorthand and typewriting.

But just try the same thing with the imagination! You will soon see that comparisons cannot be made, for no one can determine whether his own imagery is better, more artistic, and above all more plastic than that of another.

Of course, there are exceptions. No one will deny that Jules Verne was one of the most imaginatively gifted men who ever lived. He described not only aeroplanes but even submarines in definite terms at a time when the human mind was far from making any of the "dreams of the future" workable.

There is no doubt that authors who write Utopian romances have rich imaginations. On the other hand, it does not follow that people who do not or cannot write such romances have poor imaginations. We can only estimate the quality of a person's imagination, however, if he has given us concrete evidence of it. And as this is not often possible, it is safe to say that: It is impossible to make comparisons in the faculty of imagination—barring a very few exceptions—and it is not a simple matter to determine whether a person has a good imagination or not. Mnemonics alone can decide it, and we will take up that subject later.

In developing the memory, a "vivid imagination" is a very desirable acquisition. I consider it necessary to state this axiom emphatically because we generally ascribe an "imaginative nature" to the person who is completely wrapped up in day-dreams and accomplishes nothing in life.

Now, while a man who lives only in his dream world cannot measure up to the realities and exigencies of life, on the other hand it is good for a person occasionally, but not for too long a time, to surrender himself to day-dreams. It is a psychological truism, generally acknowledged since the days of Coué and Baudouin, that every concept in the human brain works toward its own fruition.

For instance, an employee in a company imagines that the business belongs to him and that he is the head of the firm. This goal seems worth working for, else it would not figure in his imagination. But when he comes to think of minor details connected with this "castle in the air," he begins to consider how he would run the business, what changes he would make, what he would expect of his employees and the like. This last thought strikes rather close to home. Is he, as an employee, fulfilling the duties he would as head of the house demand of his employees? Meditation of this sort can yield very practical results, for he may make important changes in his routine.

Thinking about how *he* would conduct the business may lead him to discover improvements which need not remain imaginary but may be put into practice and made to pay. He can pass along these discoveries, which are largely the product of his imagination, to his superior, and there is always the possibility that he will be promoted more rapidly.

We can assert quite generally that people lacking in imagination fail to get ahead in the world because they do not have the ability to picture themselves climbing the ladder of success. But imagination is equally necessary for the proper functioning of our memories. And this is the reason why I have been so explicit in discussing it.

To the question I am frequently called on to answer— whether it is possible to improve and cultivate the imagination—I should answer Yes.

The exercises which I suggested for sharpening the powers of observation are suitable for stimulating the imagination when the matter under consideration is one of recalling observed happenings. The reproduction of pictures seen, architectural details, etc., also sharpens the imagination since it is always necessary to visualise what one has seen before one can reproduce it.

Here is an even better exercise: Imagine that certain historical events or personal experiences for some important reason or other had been altered in their course.

That sounds rather theoretical, but in reality it is quite simple. For instance, think of the Battle of Hastings and ask yourself what would have happened if a victorious Harold had driven the Normans back into the sea. You call to mind Harold's success against the Danes at Stamford Bridge, and how William the Conqueror ravaged the country from Humber to Tweed. You remember the Domesday Book, in which William recorded all the lands of England with details of their cultivation, etc. What would Harold have done in his place had he been spared to continue his reign? Of course, an experiment of this kind calls for a rather wide knowledge of history and personalities. Naturally it is always simpler to choose your own personal experiences and make yourself the centre of your conjectures.

Say you recently had a business conference which did not turn out to your liking. Now imagine that the result was as you wished it and picture to yourself, as graphically as you can, what you would have gained personally or professionally. Such an exercise will not only develop your imagination but also help you to think of arguments that you can put up successfully at a similar conference in the future.

In the final analysis, however, the cultivation of the imagination should serve to make visual association of ideas easier. We know, naturally, that our memory, even without special aid, retains visual associations best and longest. Later we shall see what valuable services mnemotechny renders to such associations of ideas.

CHAPTER VII

THE LAWS OF ASSOCIATION AND THE CHAIN METHOD

WE have seen that the pictorial association of ideas fails when it comes to abstract ideas. Of course, it fails grievously when it is no longer a question of nouns but of qualifying adjectives. The concepts "hot" and "eager" can be expressed visually only indirectly through nouns to which they are related so closely that to recall the one is to recall the other.

We must, therefore, have various methods of connecting ideas to choose from, and we want, above all, to take into consideration those persons whose imaginations are unable to make mental pictures of thought-connections. The advantage of mastering a variety of methods of making connecting links between mental concepts is obvious.

Whenever you hear the name Julius Caesar you immediately think of the Roman invasion of Britain; and when you hear of the Roman invasion of Britain you think of Julius Caesar. The same thing holds true when you hear the date 55 B.C., for all three concepts are so closely connected in the minds of educated Englishmen that recalling one immediately recalls the others.

When conversation turns to the Battle of Britain, most people immediately think of the Royal Air Force, and again the reverse of this holds true. When you hear the words Magna Carta you immediately think of King

John, and when the invention of printing is mentioned, of William Caxton.

From these examples it is apparent that there are concepts which are so closely connected (that is, associated in our minds) that one habitually calls forth the other. Even the ancients recognised the importance of such connections for every sort of memory. Aristotle laid down four fundamental laws applying to thought-association:

1. Likeness (similarity)
2. Contrast
3. Contiguity in space
4. Contiguity in time

We call these connections *association-laws*. What is meant by association-laws can be explained by a simple example:

The connection between two Inter-City Euston – Piccadilly expresses of British Rail is likeness-association because both belong among the fastest trains in the country, both are restaurant-car trains, and both run between London and Manchester.

The association between either of these trains and any goods train is contrast-association, since no greater antithesis can be imagined than the fast passenger train and the slower goods train carrying coal or other bulky loads.

When a train heading for Manchester meets its London-bound counterpart, the association is through contiguity in space since they are both in approximately the same spot. That they are not actually contiguous is naturally beside the point.

Were the train to leave Manchester at the same time that another train left London, the association would be through contiguity in time. If for some reason or other the travelling time of one of the two trains is to be remembered, the travelling time of the other (which, of course, would have to be known beforehand) would furnish a check. Perfect coincidence in time is naturally as unnecessary as "actual contiguity." It is sufficient for the application of association-laws if the time of travelling is approximately the same for both trains.

Modern psychology and philosophy have extended these ideas in certain respects and narrowed them in others, but we can disregard fine theoretical distinctions because this book has been written for practical use and for the practical work of the mind.

Books of modern times dealing with association-laws, for instance those by Loisette and Poehlmann, are divided as follows in respect to the differences in concepts from a purely practical point of view:

1. Synonyms. Words of similar meaning such as *lady, woman, wife* or *zealous, eager, industrious*.

2. Similarity of sound. Words which may rhyme, but not necessarily, such as *wall, fall, call, mall, ball, pall*, or *haste* and *taste*.

3. The whole and a part. For instance, *man* and *eye, room* and *chair, book* and *page*.

4. Things of the same species. For instance, *rose* and *carnation* (both are flowers), *cannon* and *bomb* (both are offensive weapons), *chair* and *table* (both are furniture).

When this association-law should be employed we think: "Both are . . ."

5. Species and kind. For instance, *human being* and *Indian*. Every Indian is a human being, but not every human being is an Indian. *Furniture* and *table;* every table is a piece of furniture but not every piece of

furniture is a table. *Weapon* and *pistol*; every pistol is a weapon, but not every weapon is a pistol.

6. Cause and effect. For instance, *alcohol* and *drunkenness*. Drinking alcohol leads to drunkenness. *Sun* and *heat*; the sun radiates heat. *Murder* and *retribution*; committing murder is the cause of retribution.

7. Contrasts. For instance, *man* and *wife*, *light* and *dark*, *industrious* and *lazy*, etc.

8. Matching pairs. For instance, *penholder* and *penpoint*, *student* and *book*, *wall* and *picture*, etc.

9. Subject and quality. For instance, *sun* and *hot*, *stone* and *heavy*, *grandfather* and *old*. Under this association-law we relate persons or things with qualities which are peculiarly their own.

It is obvious that this compilation can be extended, but the cited examples are sufficient for practical purposes. But there is one more association-law which should be added because it plays an important part in everyday life and especially because I have found it eminently helpful in memorising facts. It is this:

10. The accidental association of a concept, which can be either objective or subjective.

The association is objective in the case of all historical events, notably in the examples I quoted at the beginning of this chapter—King John and Magna Carta, Caxton and the discovery of printing.

Had Caxton died in infancy, he would not have become the first English printer and no association between the two concepts could be made. But since the first book to be printed in English was printed by Caxton, and since every educated person knows about this, so close an association exists between the two concepts that the thought of one always calls forth the thought of the other.

The same thing happens in the case of King John and the signing of Magna Carta. So here we are concerned with accidental associations that are objective; that is, those that are valid for everyone, not only for the readers of this book.

Now let us take this example: If your umbrella were lost on a number 85 bus, you personally would form an association between the two concepts *umbrella* and *number 85 bus.* The thought of one would call to mind the thought of the other, but this association would hold true only for you and would not exist for others.

Enough of theory. For the application of these association-laws, as you will see, is not a theoretical matter at all, but an eminently practical one. To prove my point, I present a great array of concepts, to which we shall apply association-laws by joint effort. But, for your own sake, *use the association-laws I suggest only after you have tried to find the suitable ones yourself.*

It is often doubtful which law to apply. *Man* and *wife* can be considered under "matching pairs" as well as under "contrasts." Which one is the better depends upon the context in which these words appear. So it is not absolutely necessary for you to choose the association-law I myself choose. However, it is necessary for you to choose the law that actually suits the two words. You will soon see why.

We begin with **school** and **child** and easily find the association-law of "matching pairs." Then take **child** and **memory**. "The whole and a part" suits this idea best, because memory is, of course, a function of the brain. **Memory and mnemotechny:** "cause and effect," for mnemotechny helps to develop the memory. **Mnemotechny and knowledge:** "the whole and a part," since mnemotechny is a branch of the whole field of knowledge. **Knowledge and student:** "matching pairs," because the student should apply himself to gaining knowledge. **Student and lecture hall:** again "matching pairs," since the student spends much of his time in the lecture hall. **Lecture hall and acoustics:** "subject and quality," because good acoustics are usually found in lecture halls. **Acoustical and visual:** "contrast," because we know that people are apt to be either acoustical (ear-minded) or visual (eye-minded). **Visual and book:** "matching pairs," for the eye-minded learns best from reading a book.

And now, start with the word **school** and recall what idea you associate with it. I am absolutely sure that the word **child** occurred to you, and I am just as sure that you will connect the concept **memory** with the word **child** without even thinking about it. In short, you are able to build up the whole series of concepts from memory without any conscious effort on your part to impress the words on your mind.

This result is, of course, based on the hypothesis that you have chosen your association-laws as I requested, instead of merely reading those I suggested. But if you did not heed my advice, you cheated yourself of the pleasure and surprise of repeating effortlessly this entire series.

The reason why this experiment was so successful, although you did not "learn" the words in sequence, was because you were unconsciously forced, in your search for the association-law, to concentrate on the two important concepts in question though only for a short while. Because this short while was correctly utilised it was sufficient to impress the words in your memory without effort and in fact without intention on your part.

From this you can see what far-reaching consequences this experiment promises for your memory.

But for the present it is enough for us to realise that this method can be used to great advantage in making addresses, without constantly referring to a manuscript. Nothing is more exasperating than reading an address from a manuscript. You can learn the right method for delivering an address entirely from memory, using merely a few cue words as aids to memory.

The words which we have just impressed on our minds with the help of association-laws were not chosen at random, but can serve as cue words for the introduction of an address on "The Cultivation of the Memory." This address might run as follows:

"Modern **school** methods for training the memory leave much to be desired. In school the **child** is almost always told what he must learn without having been taught how he should learn it. And too little attention is paid to the fact that the **memory** functions differently in different pupils. Consequently not only general aids but individual helps which must be given if pupils are to learn anything are overlooked. Such aids to learning are provided in superior degree by **mnemotechnical** methods since they not only facilitate study in individual cases, but by and large help to develop everyone's memory. More attention should be paid to these methods outside school, too; this especially should hold true for those who follow professions for a livelihood.

"All **knowledge** is worth while not only for its own sake but for the subject-matter it furnishes the mind, and therefore we should, of course, not be indifferent to whether or not this matter is remembered systematically and logically. It follows that no **student** should neglect acquainting himself with the basic principles of mnemotechny and applying them to his profession. Quite apart from all other benefits it is a matter of common sense for him to find out what advantages they may afford him in the **lecture hall** and in his classes. If he is **acoustical** (ear-minded) the sound waves which reach his ears will make a deeper impression than they will on the **visual** (eye-minded) student. The former will therefore benefit more by attending lectures, preferring them to study from **books,** while with the latter the opposite is true."

When you read this list of words and the address in which they are used, the great help this method offers will not be quite apparent to you. But let a few days elapse without looking again at the chain of words or the address.

After two or three days test yourself, find out how many of the words and how much of the address you still remember. You will be amazed when you see for yourself that you remember considerably more than you are accustomed to demand from your memory. If you again wait for a few days, say a week, and once more test your memory, you will find that you can recite the chain and the address from memory without a mistake.

THE PRACTICAL APPLICATION OF THE CHAIN METHOD

In order to show how the chain method may be applied in a practical way, I have selected the following speech made by Winston Churchill:

(1) "Now the war has come, and when it is over **let us** be careful **not** to **make the same mistake** or the same sort of mistake **as Germany made** when she had France prostrate at her feet **in 1870. Let us,** whatever we do, **fight for and work toward** great and **sound principles for the European system.** And **the first of these principles** which should be kept before us is **the**

principle of nationality—that is to say, **not the conquest** or subjugation **of any great community** or of any strong race of men, **but the setting free of those races** which have been subjugated and conquered; and if doubt arises about disputed areas of country we should try to **settle** their ultimate destination in **the reconstruction of Europe** which must follow from this war **with a fair regard to** the wishes and feelings of **the people** who live in them.

(2) "That is **the aim,** which if it is achieved **will justify the exertions** of the war and will **make some amends** to the world **for the loss and suffering,** the agony of suffering, which it has brought and entailed, and which will **give** to those who come after us **not only the pride** which we hope they will feel **in** remembering the **material achievements** of the present age of Britain **but** which will give them **also a better and fairer world** to live in **and a Europe free from the causes of hatred** and unrest which have poisoned the comity of nations and ruptured the peace of Christendom."

Let us try to remember this inspiring speech by using the chain method. To make the task easier and to show how to proceed in order to remember these two paragraphs, I have numbered them, and I have underlined the cue words; now I shall enumerate these cue words in order to remind us of the leading thoughts in the speech. While you read this chain, you can check the cue words with the respective paragraphs of the speech to which they belong:

(1) let us not make the same mistake
    as Germany made in 1870
    Let us fight for and work toward

    sound principles for the European system
    the first of these principles
    the principle of nationality
    not the conquest of any great community
    but the setting free of races
    settle the reconstruction of Europe
    with a fair regard to the people
(2) the aim will justify the exertions
    make some amends for the loss and suffering
    give not only the pride in material achievements
    but also a better and fairer world
    and a Europe free from the causes of hatred

Before we try to repeat the speech, we ask ourselves whether we know exactly which thought each of the cue words represents, and how each thought is linked to the following thought. Let us try the first paragraph together:

The first thought is: "Let us not make the same mistake." This naturally raises the question: "What mistake?" The answer is given by the second thought. Then, having warned us against what we should not do, the speech goes on to state what we should do. This is the third thought: "Fight and work." For what? For sound principles for the European system. What is the first of these principles? It is the principle of nationality. What does this mean? The seventh thought explains what it doesn't mean as a preliminary to the next thought, which tells us what it does mean. This explanation is enlarged upon in the last two thoughts of the first paragraph. In this way we see how the train of thought in the first paragraph naturally hangs together and this helps us to remember this part of the speech.

In the second paragraph I start with "the aim," and ask: "What will it do?" Answer: "It will justify the exertions of the war." What else? It will make some amends for the loss and suffering. What else will it do? It will also give: (a) pride in material achievements; (b) a better and fairer world; and (c) a Europe free from the causes of hatred.

If you follow the reasoning for these two paragraphs, you will see that you can repeat the contents of the speech in less than twenty minutes. And it will stay in your memory for years and years. Of course, we shall use the many cue words indicated here only if we intend to repeat the speech verbatim. If we content ourselves with the leading thoughts, we should use not more than one or two cue words or phrases for each paragraph, and the chain would be like this:

(1) let us fight for and work toward
    the setting free of races
(2) the aim will make amends for loss and suffering and give
    a Europe free from the causes of hatred.

The more in detail we wish to remember the original, the more cue words are necessary, and no general rules can be given as to their number. Although we used about fifteen cue words or phrases to repeat all the thoughts in the speech, we could make the same number suffice for remembering the contents of an entire book, if we limited ourselves to a general résumé of it.

What results we can achieve in developing our memories is illustrated in a striking way by those cases of memory geniuses, of which there have been some outstanding examples, particularly in the history of this country.

For example, the English historian Thomas Babington Macaulay (1800-1859) could read a page or a chapter once only and repeat it from memory. He was able rapidly to memorise the contents of a book and repeat them almost without a mistake. He is said to have learned the entire New Testament by heart, and to have won a bet by memorising Milton's "Paradise Lost" in a single night.

Thomas Carlyle (1795-1881), too, had a remarkable memory which stood him in good stead when a maid-servant accidentally destroyed the first draft of his book *The French Revolution.* On learning of the loss of the manuscript he sat down and drew upon his memory to rewrite it.

Blaise Pascal (1623-1662), the French writer and theologian, was complete master of the contents of the Bible, and could instantly repeat any passage, giving its context as well as chapter and verse.

The ease with which Joseph Addison (1672-1719), the essayist of "Spectator" fame, recited from memory selections from writers both ancient and modern aroused the wonder and admiration of his friends.

These instances, recorded of men who knew more about the working of memory than most of their contemporaries, are cited to illustrate some of the outstanding feats which our memory, when developed and strengthened, like a muscle in the human body, by proper training, is capable of accomplishing.

CHAPTER VIII

CLASSIFICATION AS A MEANS OF ASSOCIATION

CLASSIFIED material is easier to remember than is unclassified material. This statement is so obvious that one would assume everyone knows it.

A writer, we should suppose, in preparing a book for publication organises his material as logically as possible, just as a student bent on studying brings his material into some sort of order. A glance at our literature, however, and a few questions put to students or apprentices show that this theoretical recognition of a trite statement is not actually carried out in practice.

Let us try an experiment with a simple example. Look at the following illustration, which shows twelve objects. Study it for a while and then put the book aside and try to recall all twelve objects.

When you have finished this exercise, consider the second illustration. You will find it shows exactly the same objects, this time arranged in four groups. Each group contains three objects which have been selected because they have a general relationship among themselves.

bottle	cigarette box
glass	cigarette lighter
table-mat	ash tray
magazine	pen
newspaper	pencil
book	eraser

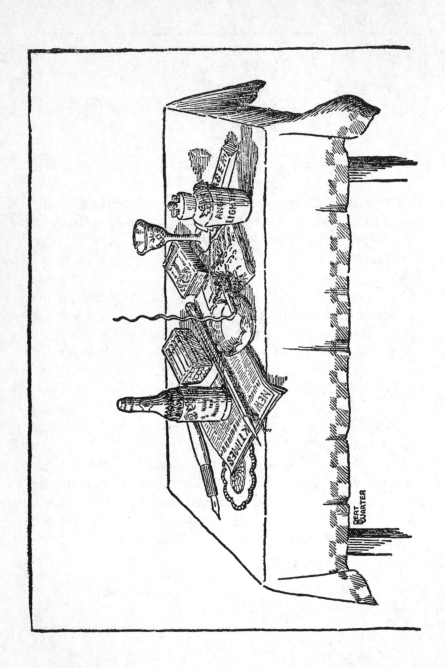

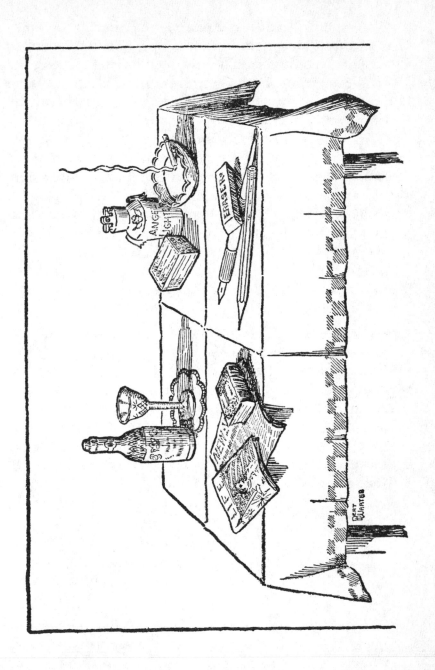

As you will readily concede, the time it takes to memorise the objects in the second illustration is less than half the time required for memorising those in the first, even though there are twelve objects in each drawing and even though the twelve objects are the same in both pictures.

And the principle which is valid for these simple objects is also valid for the complicated matters of business life. I would even go a step further and assert that the more difficult and complex the affairs of a business which we would like to have at our finger-tips, the more desirable it is to make such groupings and sub-groupings. We call this grouping *classification*.

Here are a few examples from various kinds of businesses which I have selected at random from technical books:

For the timber industry there is, for instance, a hand-book entitled *Tested Selling Methods*. In this booklet the methods which make the selling of building material easier and more profitable are presented and illustrated clearly and well. A primer in the same field also is published. From these two books I see that the timber dealer who estimates for the building of a house must set up certain specifications which have the following basic elements:

Exterior walls	Windows
Framing	Doors
Roofing	Cupboards
Interior walls	Insulation
Flooring	Heating equipment
Joinery	Plumbing

Naturally these specifications are familiar to the timber dealer. But we are not concerned with those persons who have already reached the top rung of the ladder in their field, but with the man who is still at the bottom and who must absorb into his memory the knowledge he needs to advance. For such an individual the sequence we are concerned with is not an easy one to retain. So let us try grouping and sub-grouping this material.

To begin with, every house consists of the following parts: outside, inside, and fixtures. The outside consists of the exterior walls, framing, and roofing. The inside includes the interior walls, flooring, and joinery; and, as fixtures, heating and plumbing equipment. We group windows, doors, and cupboards under the heading of joinery. Thus, without effort, we get the following table:

OUTSIDE	INSIDE	FIXTURES
Exterior walls	Interior walls	Plumbing
Framing	Flooring	Insulation
Roofing	Joinery	Heating equipment
	Windows	
	Doors	
	Cupboards	

As you see, the task of remembering has been made considerably easier by the aid of this classification. Using the table rather than simple enumeration makes an overall comprehension of the specifications much easier. We now have four groups, each of which consists of three items. Even the person who has no possible interest in the timber industry can make a simple test to prove to himself how easy it is to remember such a grouping. Try it. After a few days during which you have not thought about the subject, see if you can reconstruct the table. You will be surprised at the ease with which you can enumerate all twelve items without a single mistake.

And here is another example, likewise dealing with the timber industry:

A firm issued a manual called *Net Profit Guide and Operating Chart for Retail Timber and Building Material Executives.* According to the preface this book, unique of its kind, "identifies, charts, and implements those principles, policies, and techniques of building material retailing which have demonstrated repeatedly their net profit producing power." It is the result of several years of research work and was prepared for the exclusive benefit of executives. Through the kind permission of this firm, I quote the excerpts which follow.

In this book "the ten major elements of net profit have been segregated into ten divisions, and these divisions have been listed in the proper sequence for most effective action." From this material, assembled and thoroughly tested through long years of experience, I choose pages 29-31 at random and find there a section called "Getting the Most from Operating Man-Power":

1. I will check full and proper use of time by all employees.
2. I will provide a job analysis and responsibility chart for each operating employee.
3. I will establish timing, co-ordination and correlation in my employees' work.
4. I will train employees in more effective techniques in their work.
5. I will review my compensation policies and make adjustments which will tend to increase efficiency.
6. I will install incentives to greater sales and profits wherever possible among my operating employees.
7. I will co-ordinate the training of my operating employees with my continuous training of sales employees.
8. I will check the honesty of every employee handling cash and will notify my whole organisation that this is being done frequently.

9. I will take a personal interest in each employee and evidence it occasionally.

10. I will have consistent policies on promotions, holidays, short time and dismissals and will acquaint the organisation with what they may expect.

11. I will assure myself that every employee is sales-conscious and productive.

12. I will weed out the misfits in my organisation as rapidly as possible and replace them with effective man-power.

13. I will analyse the detailed work of myself and other executives and will delegate to less highly-paid personnel all details that they can handle effectively.

14. If necessary details are burdensome (and therefore not handled correctly), I will employ an apprentice to handle many of them.

15. I will assign specific responsibility for orderliness and cleanliness to one individual.

Excellent though this section may be from the standpoint of business advice, it falls short when viewed from the angle of classification, because these fifteen points are very difficult to remember in the sequence in which they are presented.

Then, too, since the section is concerned throughout with things which the personnel manager of the firm should always bear in mind, and since it is a mere fraction of a book whose complete contents he is to remember, an orderly classification is doubly desirable.

I suggest that you yourself attempt such a classification. See if you can group several of the fifteen points under a single heading. Try to find three or four (but no more) main headings and then see if you can organise the fifteen points under those main headings. Only after you have made this attempt yourself should you look at my table, which follows. Decide which you like better, and whether or not you want to make any changes in yours or mine.

I should like to add that any classification you yourself make is bound to be more helpful to your memory. Memory works, as we have proved repeatedly, in a manner more or less peculiar to each individual, and therefore *you can retain better the material which you yourself have classified than a classification furnished by someone else.*

The following table shows the classification which I suggest. The numbers in parentheses after each line point to the number of the original sequence as printed above.

I have not made any intentional changes in the material itself, and the condensations in phraseology as used in my classification should not be construed as a desire to change the meaning of the original statements.

I. *The right man in the right job*
>   (1) Job analysis and responsibility chart (2)
>   (2) Analyse the work of executives and delegate some of it to less highly-paid personnel (13)
>   (3) If necessary, employ apprentices (14)
>   (4) Weed out the misfits (12)
>   (5) Check honesty (8)

II. *Training employees*
>   (6) Train employees in more effective techniques (4)
>   (7) Check full and proper use of time (1)
>   (8) Time and co-ordinate the work of employees (3)
>   (9) Co-ordinate the training of operating employees with the training of sales employees (7)
>   (10) Be sure that every employee is sales-conscious and productive (11)
>   (11) Assign responsibility for orderliness and cleanliness (15)

III. *Compensation*
>   (12) Review compensation policies (5)
>   (13) Install incentives to greater sales (6)

(14) Have consistent policies for promotion, etc. (10)
(15) Take a personal interest in each employee (non-
   material compensation) (9)

The irrefutable logic of this classification is proved by
the following sentences, in which the numbers in parentheses refer to my grouping and not to the original
extract:

I. *The Right Man in the Right Job*

The basic essential of good management is job analysis; that is, a study of each job and what work it entails
(1). This analysis will distribute details hitherto performed by executives among employees who are paid
smaller salaries (2), and some of the work of these latter
may then be delegated to apprentices (3). Misfits are to
be discharged (4) and the honesty of all who remain in
the firm's employ is to be checked periodically (5).

II. *Training Employees*

Employees are to be trained in the most effective
techniques (6), and care should be taken that their
working hours are used to the best advantage of the
company (7). The work of all employees is to be co-
ordinated (8); likewise, the training of all operating
employees is to be co-ordinated with the training of
sales employees (9). Every employee shall be sales-
conscious and productive (10) and orderly and present-
able (11).

III. *Compensation*

Compensation policies are to be checked periodically
(12) and incentives to greater sales and profits introduced (13). Promotions, holidays, short time, and dismissals shall be just and fair (14). In order to gauge the

worth of each individual employee fairly, a personal interest in his welfare is essential (15).

If you are convinced that such a classification is quite simple to commit to memory, you will not hesitate to introduce it in your own line of business or, should you be an employee, to apply it to any matter which you must bear in mind.

CHAPTER IX

LEARNING WORDS IN FOREIGN LANGUAGES

EVER since people began to engage in trade and commerce and thereby to come into contact with foreigners, they have had to learn the language of the country with which they wished to do business. Because acquiring a foreign language is one of the oldest branches of knowledge, one would think that during the many years which have passed a method could have been found for making the study-process easier and the learning-process more effective.

In reality, however, only the last few decades have produced a small number of volumes based on a truly rational method. Most textbooks still prefer to follow the tradition sanctified by long usage.

When we are learning a foreign language, the new words are the most important thing, and before we do anything else we must learn to translate them from our mother tongue to the new language.

The farther we progress in the foreign language, the farther into the background this linking of words recedes until finally, when we can really speak the new language well, we think in it naturally, without translating.

The usual method which the average man applies in learning a vocabulary of foreign words is that he repeats the two words one after the other until he thinks he has them fixed in mind. What is the weakness of this method? It does not take long to find it.

The human mind is so constituted that it is always looking for something new. If the vocabulary or words to be memorised are repeated one after the other in a more or less mechanical fashion, they offer nothing new for the mind to grasp. It wanders and busies itself with something else while the lips mechanically keep on murmuring the words. What happens is the exact opposite of concentration. It is a direct invitation to wool-gathering, for such absent-mindedness really ensues when we try to learn something yet at the same time let our minds be occupied by something else.

Poehlmann points out, quite correctly, that Latin textbooks for beginners usually introduce *farmer-agricola* early in the course. The student must keep impressing this word on his mind by the usual process of repetition until it sticks. How much easier it is for the student to learn that *acre* is *ager*, aided by the similarity in sound of the two words. If in addition he has learned that to *cultivate* is *colere*, no extra time or thought need be spent on the compounded word *agri-cola* (*ager colere*).

This example is but one of thousands which could be cited from foreign-language textbooks.

It is more logical and to the point for anyone who wants to learn a foreign tongue to study first of all those words which are spelled the same, or nearly the same, in his own language. In English-German there are, for instance:

> rose—die Rose
> ring—der Ring
> gold—das Gold
> grass—das Gras
> rust—der Rost
> man—der Mann

Then follow the words which, while differing in spelling, yet have a fairly similar sound:

> steel—der Stahl
> moon—der Mond
> father—der Vater
> come—kommen

Whether such words are few or many depends upon the degree of relationship between one's own language and the particular foreign one.

If thought-associations like those given above cannot be made, that is, if the foreign word sounds entirely different from the same word in our own language, we can lighten our task of learning it by employing linking words.

Naturally this plan again offers various possibilities. The simplest and most effective is to find a linking word in one's own language, a word which in *meaning* is similar to the given word but in *sound* resembles the foreign word to be learned. If we go back to the Latin, we find the following example:

In Latin, *hand* is *manus*. In English, we have the word *manufacturer*, originally someone who made something by hand. If we therefore insert *manufacturer* as the linking word between *hand* and *manus*, we use this chain of thought: I am trying to think of the Latin word for *hand*. *Hand* reminds me of the man who makes something by hand or causes it to be made by hand, therefore *manufacturer*. If I know this word, I can easily recall the Latin word *manus*.

Another example: To *know* is *cognoscere* in Latin. These are entirely different words, and there is apparently no connection between the two. But if I *know* someone I can say I *recognise* him. This word is so similar to the Latin term I am trying to think of that memorising the latter offers no further difficulty.

There is a twofold advantage in learning words in this way:

First, stupid, parrot-like repetition is done away with. The habit of endless repetition, as I have pointed out, tends to destroy concentration.

Secondly, terms learned by the method I have outlined make a much deeper impression and remain in the memory much longer, once they are learned. The reader cannot check this assertion offhand; but try to learn foreign terms with the aid of a modern textbook or by inserting your own linking words and you will shortly see how astonishingly well you remember them.

Now, of course, there are a great number of terms for which it is impossible to find linking words as closely related in meaning to the words in one's own language as the cited examples.

In spite of this fact we need not discard our method. Basing my conclusions on an extensive study of many languages, I have found that in almost all instances, it is possible to discover a word in our own language that is similar in sound to the foreign word. Once I know such a word, with a little practice in inserting linking words I can make a connection in my own language whenever a natural connection does not exist.

The following examples demonstrate this point:

The English word *tomb* is entirely dissimilar and has no relationship to the German words *das Grabmal*. But it is easy to form a connection betweeen *tomb* and *grave*, and the latter word sounds so much like the German words *das Grab*, that remembering it presents no difficulty.

Since actual practice is much more instructive than

theory, I shall present a series of examples, emphasising the fact that the etymology of the words is entirely beside the point. I assume that the etymology of the word is *unknown* to the reader, for if it is known, we can naturally dispense with mnemotechnical aids.

Examples for English-French:

top	summit	le sommet
woman	feminine	la femme
share	part	la part
danger	risk	le risque
insanity	demented	la démence
middle	centre	le centre
busy	occupied	occupé
death	mortal	la mort
house	mason	la maison
news	novel	la nouvelle
noon	midday	le midi
mail	post	la poste
song	chant	la chanson
speed	rapid	la rapidité
food	nourishment	la nourriture
duty	function	la fonction
clock	hour	une horloge
shadow	umbrella	une ombre
ear	aural	une oreille

Examples for English-German:

basement	cellar	der Keller
cloakroom	wardrobe	die Garderobe
tomb	grave	das Grabmal
merchandise	ware	die Ware
duty	toll	der Zoll
soft	weak	weich
assist	help	helfen
boy	young	der Junge
dog	hound	der Hund

savage	barbarian	der Barbar
letter	brief	der Brief (a brief letter)
flower	bloom	die Blume
flour	meal	das Mehl
enemy	fiend	der Feind
meat	flesh	das Fleisch
road	way	der Weg
carpet	tapestry	der Teppich
table	dish	der Tisch
shave	razor	rasieren

Examples for English-Spanish:

child	infant	el infante
horse	cavalry	el caballo
door	portal	la puerta
heart	core	el corazón
mind	mental	la mente
neck	collar	el cuello
at once	prompt	pronto
prize	premium	el premio
table	mess	la mesa
knife	cut	el cuchillo
scale	balance	la balanza
wages	salary	el salario
untruth	false	la falsedad
star	stellar	la estrella

Examples from English-Latin:

home	domicile	domus
big	magnify	magnus
peace	pacts	pax
chief	principal	princeps
king	reign	rex
slave	serve	servus
life	vital	vita
light	luminous	lux
shelter	protection	tectum

From experience I know that at first glance this method of learning terms will seem odd to many of my readers. Put it to the test of actual practice, however, before forming an opinion.

Just make the following experiment: In the next few days learn one or two hundred foreign words by the method you usually employ: in the following few days learn the same number in the same language (naturally different words) by the method I have outlined, that is, by the insertion of linking words of your own choosing. Then let the whole thing alone for a week or two, without even thinking about it.

After about two weeks see how many words you remember of those you learned by the old method and how many you learned by the new method of employing linking words.

I can tell you in advance that the latter figure is sure to be 100 or 200 per cent higher, that is, you will have remembered at least twice as many words, perhaps even three or four times as many as you learned by the old method.

Remember that everything new first meets with opposition and that every forward step is apt to be greeted with a headshake. That is only human.

When railway trains were invented and the first train was to swoop along at the then unheard-of speed of twenty miles an hour, the Prussian Academy of Medicine proclaimed that no one could suffer such speed without going crazy, and in all seriousness demanded that a high wooden fence be erected along the entire length of the track, so that innocent bystanders would not be scared out of their wits by the sight of the madly speeding monster.

It took Gillette many years to convince men that his razor is safer than the old-fashioned blade. Dozens of illustrations come to mind, all proving that the new always meets with opposition. In the present instance, you have a great advantage over Gillette: You need invest no money, build no factories, nor the like. You have only to make an experiment with your own mind before you come to a decision on the matter.

CHAPTER X

REMEMBERING THE COUNTIES AND THEIR ADMINISTRATIVE CENTRES

OUR next problem is to learn how to master names which are especially difficult to remember and for which we cannot easily find meaningful words of similar sound. How shall we set about memorising, by a simple method, a rather long, collective series of difficult names? As a concrete example, let us take the forty-odd counties of England.

There are some people, of course, who visualise the map so clearly that they can name the counties according to their geographical location, that is, reel off their names as though reading from an actual map. A person who can do this naturally does not need any special aid, which should be employed only when certain facts are hard or impossible to retain naturally. But even these persons will find it worth while to read the solution of this problem carefully, because the same method can be used for all sorts of other things difficult to memorise.

First of all, write down the complete list of names serially—in this instance, the counties of England. Beside each county write words of similar sound which have a sensible meaning. The degree of similarity in sound is an individual matter. For the person who relies greatly on such aid the sound must be very like that of the word to be memorised.

The relationship here resembles that of actor and prompter. The actor who knows his part pretty well needs to be prompted only occasionally, but the actor who is just beginning to learn his lines has to rely on the prompter during the whole performance.

Taking an example at random, we can illustrate this with Bedfordshire. The word nearest in sound to Bedfordshire perhaps is **bedlam.** Then there are **bed, bedding,** and **bedouin.** These do not completely exhaust the possibilities, and you may be able to think of a few more.

Going down the list of counties in this way, we have something like the following:

1. Avon   avenue.
2. Bedfordshire   bed, bedding, bedlam, bedouin.
3. Berkshire   bark, barked.
4. Buckinghamshire   buccaneer, buck, bucket, buckler, buckram, buckshee.
5. Cambridgeshire   cambric, came.
6. Cheshire   chess, chest, chesterfield, chestnut.
7. Cleveland   cleavage, cleave, cleaver.
8. Cornwall   corn, cornea, corner, cornet, corn-flower, cornice, cornucopia.
9. Cumbria   come, cumber, cumbersome, cummerbund.
10. Derbyshire   Derby, darbies, Darby and Joan.
11. Devonshire   devil.
12. Dorset   dorsal, door-sill, indoors.
13. Durham   endure.
14. East Sussex   easy suspects.
15. Essex   essay, essence, essential, sex.
16. Gloucestershire gloss, glossy, glossary.
17. Greater London   great luncheon.
18. Greater Manchester great man's chest.
19. Hampshire   ham, hammer, hamper, hamster, hamstring.
20. Hereford &
    Worcester   herring worsted.
21. Hertfordshire   heart, hearth, heartily, heartless, hearty.

22. Humberside	humble side.
23. Kent	ken, Ken, kennel.
24. Lancashire	language, lank, lanky.
25. Leicestershire	less, lessen, lesser, lesson, lest.
26. Lincolnshire	link, links.
27. Merseyside	murky side.
28. Norfolk	nor.
29. Northamptonshire	north.
30. Northumberland	northward.
31. North Yorkshire	nor yours.
32. Nottinghamshire	knot, knotting, not.
33. Oxfordshire	ox, oxide, Oxo, oxygen.
34. Salop	slap, slip, slippy, sloop, slop, slope, sloppy.
35. Somerset	some, somersault, sum, summary, summer, summit, summon.
36. South Yorkshire	soothe yours.
37. Staffordshire	staff.
38. Suffolk	suffer, suffering, suffix, suffocate.
39. Surrey	Norroy, surrender, surreptitious, surrogate.
40. Tyne & Wear	tiny weir.
41. Warwickshire	warrant, warren, warrior.
42. West Midlands	midst.
43. West Sussex	waste such eggs.
44. West Yorkshire	waste yours.
45. Wiltshire	will, wilt.

We are not trying to memorise the counties in any particular order. Our problem is merely to associate substituting words for the individual counties, naturally one word for each county. The simplest way is to make up a nonsense story incorporating one of these key words for each county. Such a story might read:

The <u>avenue</u> was <u>bedlam</u> when dogs <u>barked</u> and a <u>bucket</u> <u>came</u> off the <u>chest</u> with a <u>cleaver</u> in the <u>corner</u>. <u>Cumbersome</u> <u>darbies</u> are the <u>devil</u> to <u>endure</u> <u>indoors</u> on <u>easy</u> <u>suspects</u> who <u>essay</u> to <u>gloss</u> over their <u>humble side</u>. A <u>great</u> <u>luncheon</u> <u>hamper</u> rests on a <u>great</u> <u>man's</u> <u>chest</u>.

His **herring worsted** is **not heartily kenned** after a **language lesson** on the **links. Nor** is the **murky side north** or **northward, nor yours** a **sloppy Oxo** in **summer** to **soothe yours,** who **suffer** your **staff** to **surrender** a **tiny weir** when **midst** a **warrant** which **will** not only **waste such eggs** but **waste yours.**

The names of all forty-odd counties are in this "story." Every **bold-face** word was chosen from the key words previously given.

As you will see, this little piece of nonsense can be memorised merely by reading it through four or five times. It will take only ten or fifteen minutes if you have improved your memory steadily by doing our exercises. It usually takes hours to memorise the names of the forty-odd counties, and anything learned so tediously and arbitrarily is apt to be forgotten in a few weeks or months. The little story quoted here is so easy to remember that you run no risk of forgetting it.

But let me again remind the reader: one remembers best the stories he invents himself. If you would like to remember the counties, I suggest that you make up a story yourself, using the key words given above or others of your own choosing. You will remember this story more easily because your own creative activity is involved.

Now that you have memorised the counties, suppose you continue by mastering their administrative centre names. Because we remember those things best which have meaning in themselves, we choose substituting words for the local centre as well as the counties. The factors we have considered before hold true for these words too, that is, the more nearly they sound like the original word and the more simply they can be connected in meaning with the original word, the better they are.

Of course, there is no need to carry out this process with such centres whose names can be derived from the name of the county itself, e.g., Leicestershire—Leicester. Rather let us begin with any other county which differs in name from its administrative centre.

This is Berkshire. Berks. administrative centre is Reading. Reading reminds us of red, and the key word for Berkshire is bark. Red and bark are closely connected in our minds because red setters bark, or because a red bark is a kind of evergreen tree, or because redcaps may bark orders, or because redwood trees have bark. So we can easily impress the following on our memories:

Berkshire—bark—red—Reading.

Here are some further examples:

Buckinghamshire—bucket—bucket of ale—Aylesbury.
Cornwall—cornflower—blue—true—Truro.
Cumbria—come—come by car—Carlisle.
Devonshire—devil—exorcise—Exeter.
Essex—sex—rake—take the helm—Chelmsford.
Hampshire—hammer—rifle—winchester rifle—Winchester.
Kent—kennel kennel-maid—Maidstone.
Lancashire—language—the Press—Preston.
Merseyside—murky side—murky pool—Liverpool.
Northumberland — northward — N.E.W.S. — Newcastle-upon-Tyne.
North Yorkshire—nor yours—nor all—Northallerton.
Shropshire—Shrove—Shrove-Tuesday—Shrewsbury.
Somerset—summer school—taught—Taunton.
Surrey—Norroy—Norroy King of Arms—Kingston-upon-Thames.
West Midlands—midst—midst wolves—Wolverhampton.
Wiltshire—wilt—wilt thou—Trowbridge.

The associations suggested here are so easy to formulate that further explanations are unnecessary.

CHAPTER XI

REMEMBERING THE SOVEREIGNS OF ENGLAND

EVERY Englishman should know the names of the kings and queens of England, but our task becomes more involved when we attempt to remember names in a definite, unchangeable order. The little story in the preceding chapter illustrated how much easier the task of memorising is when we are completely free in using our substituting words in a composition.

In learning the sovereigns of England we have no such freedom, for in this case a serial order is the most important factor. While this restriction makes composition of the story a little more difficult, it does not affect the system itself.

First we list the sovereigns and, where possible or necessary, find substitute words for their names, a process which need not be explained again. Then we work out a story embodying these substitute words just as we did in the case of the counties, except that in this instance we must use them in historical order.

One difficulty arises: many names are repeated several times, such as the Henrys from I to VIII, the Georges from I to VI, etc. In order to overcome this difficulty, we translate the ordinal number following the name into a letter, employing a numerical code which will be explained in Chapter XIV, and we add this letter to the abbreviation of the name itself.

This abbreviation must be formed in such a way that as few letters as possible are used; in other words, no more than are absolutely necessary for recognising the name without the possibility of error.

If the name starts with a vowel, like Edward, the E alone is enough, since there is no other English king's name which starts with an E. (I do not use abbreviations for the two queens, Elizabeth I and II.)

If the name starts with a consonant followed by a vowel, we use both these letters. **William**, therefore becomes **wi.** If it is **William I,** we add the letter **t,** thus forming the word **wit.** If it is **William II,** we add the letter **n,** thus forming the word **win** or **wins.**

However, we may enlarge our choice of words to make our associations easier. Instead of **wit,** we can also use a word like **witty.** Instead of **win,** we can also use a word like **winter,** or the like.

A variety in the choice of words facilitates associations. On the other hand, there is no danger of confusion, since we know that the first letters up to the first vowel indicate the name, whereas the following consonant indicates the ordinal number, regardless of the length of the word.

In the following "story" the words in bold-face indicate the names of the monarchs, one sentence being allocated to each dynasty, i.e., Norman, Plantagenet, Lancastrian, Yorkist, Tudor, Stuart, Hanoverian and Windsor.

Wit wins Hester. Hens rely on John for **ham,** but **Ed's enemy** an **emblem renounces. A hero's hell** is **huge. Heirs elect remember. Hectic** in **heaven etches Mary Elizabeth. Jades chat** of **Cromwell's chance** in **January** at **Wimbledon** with **Anne. Getting gen** and **gems, Germans were victors. Extra gelid** is the **effect** of **George** on **Elizabeth.**

The underlined words mean:

Norman

William I	wit
William II	wins
Henry I	He-
Stephen	-ster

Plantagenet

Henry II	hens
Richard I	rely on (*Ri*chard *Lion*heart)
John	John
Henry III	ham
Edward I	Ed
Edward II	enemy
Edward III	emblem
Richard II	renounces

Lancastrian

Henry IV	hero
Henry V	hell
Henry VI	huge

Yorkist

Edward IV	heirs (the *h* is silent)
Edward V	elect
Richard III	remember

Tudor

Henry VII	hectic
Henry VIII	heaven
Edward VI	etches
Mary	Mary
Elizabeth	Elizabeth

Stuart

James I	jades
Charles I	chat
Cromwell	Cromwell

Charles II	chance
James II	January
William III and Mary	Wimbledon
Anne	Anne

Hanoverian

George I	getting
George II	gen
George III	gems
George IV	Germans
William IV	were
Victoria	victors

Windsor

Edward VII	extra
George V	gelid
Edward VIII	effect
George VI	George
Elizabeth II	Elizabeth

This story is somewhat harder to learn than the one about the counties, because of its prescribed order. Nevertheless, one can learn this list without special effort in about an hour, while to learn the sovereigns without such aid takes much longer.

Every Englishman is expected to know not only the names of the kings and queens in chronological order but also the dates of their reigns. The latter task, too, is considerably lightened by our memory system, but before we attempt it we need further preparation. We will return to its solution in a later chapter.

CHAPTER XII

HOW TO REMEMBER NAMES AND FACES

THE lack of a reliable memory for names and faces is extremely annoying. A person whose memory for faces deserts him is often unpopular, for everyone is hurt at not being recognised. Not only will he be mortified and find himself in an awkward position, but he may even suffer financially as well.

The doctor, for instance, who fails to recognise a person on her second visit will perhaps lose her as a patient because she interprets his poor memory for faces as a lack of interest in her case.

This is equally true of the shopkeeper who fails to recognise a customer who has patronised his shop several times.

It is not altogether unreasonable for people to confuse a poor memory for names and faces with a lack of interest, for, as we have shown in the foregoing chapters, interest in a thing is one of the most important factors of memory. Nor is it a coincidence that many great men of history and literature were famous for their excellent memory for faces. That faculty, indeed, helps to explain how they attained their prominence.

It is said that Themistocles knew the 21,000 citizens of Athens by sight and by name. That this was no idle game of his is apparent when one realises how important it would be in a little democratic city-state such as Athens for each individual citizen to know he was

personally acknowledged and recognised on every occasion by the leading statesman.

A similar story is told about Napoleon. He is said to have known by name most of the soldiers in his army and to have been acquainted with their personal histories.

With the fine discernment of the poet and playwright, Shakespeare gives Hamlet a good memory not only for the faces of the players who come to perform at Elsinore but also for the lines which he has heard them speak. In Act II, Scene 2, of the tragedy he puts into Hamlet's mouth the following words:

Enter four or five Players.

You are welcome, masters; welcome all. I am glad to see thee well. Welcome, good friends. O, my old friend! thy face is valanced[1] since I saw thee last: comest thou to beard me in Denmark? What my young lady and mistress! By'r lady, your ladyship is nearer to heaven than when I saw you last, by the altitude of a chopine[2]. Pray God, your voice, like a piece of uncurrent gold, be not cracked in the ring. Masters, you are all welcome. We'll e'en to't like French falconers, fly at any thing we see: we'll have a speech straight: come, give us a taste of your quality; come, a passionate speech.

First Player. What speech, my lord?

Hamlet. I heard thee speak a speech once, but it was never acted; or, if it was, not above once; for the play, I remember, pleased not the million; 't was caviare to the general: but it was—as I received it, and others, whose judgements in such matters cried in the top of mine—an excellent play, well digested in the scenes, set down with as much modesty as cunning. I remember, one said there were no sallets[3] in the lines to make the matter savoury, nor no matter in the phrase that might

---

[1] *valanced:* bearded.
[2] *chopine:* high-heeled shoe.
[3] *sallets:* spicy bits.

indict the author of affectation; but called it an honest method, as wholesome as sweet, and by very much more handsome than fine. One speech in it I chiefly loved: 't was Aeneas' tale to Dido; and thereabout of it especially, where he speaks of Priam's slaughter: if it live in your memory, begin at this line: let me see, let me see—

"The rugged Pyrrhus, like the Hyrcanian beast",—it is not so:— it begins with Pyrrhus:—

> "The rugged Pyrrhus, he whose sable arms,
> Black as his purpose, did the night resemble
> When he lay couched in the ominous horse,
> Hath now this dread and black complexion smear'd
> With heraldry more dismal; head to foot
> Now is he total gules[1]; horridly trick'd
> With blood of fathers, mothers, daughters, sons,
> Baked and impasted with the parching streets,
> That lend a tyrannous and damned light
> To their lord's murder: roasted in wrath and fire,
> And thus o'er-sized with coagulate gore,
> With eyes like carbuncles, the hellish Pyrrhus
> Old grandsire Priam seeks."

So, proceed you.

Polonius. 'Fore God, my lord, well spoken, with good accent and good discretion.

In this passage Shakespeare has illustrated the ability of a good memory to recall faces and facts connected with them.

But we need not look to literary inventiveness for examples of a well-trained memory. History, both ancient and modern, furnishes examples of the feats achieved by geniuses of memory.

For instance, Mithridates, King of Pontus, who, as champion of the East, for eighteen years successfully

---

[1] *gules:* red.

resisted the power of Rome, possessed a most tenacious memory for names and languages. It is said that he could call each of his soldiers by name and that he could converse fluently in the twenty-two languages and dialects spoken by the people of his empire.

A case from more recent times is that of a young Dutchman known to psychologists as Peter, who knows by heart a thousand phone numbers. He concentrates on memorising personal details connected with the lives of members of the clergy. He remembers their names, initials, birthdays, when they retired, when they died, and so on. He can also make rings round anybody who tries to beat him at mental arithmetic.

If we wish to strengthen our memory for names and faces, we must first learn the prerequisite for recognising a person and then apply the rules of memory training in general, which we have discussed in earlier chapters.

If we search for the cause of our own lack of memory in this special field, we find one or more factors to account for it:

(1) Perhaps we do not remember ever having met the person, thus proving we have a bad memory for faces; or

(2) we do remember having met him but do not recall his name. This would indicate either a poor memory for names or the failure to establish a good mental association between his name and his person.

Therefore, whether we like it or not, we are forced to admit that the ability to recognise a person is based on three requirements, all of which are of equal importance and any of which may be difficult for us to meet. These three requirements are:

(1) the ability to remember a face
(2) the ability to recall a name

(3) the ability properly to connect the name with the face.

Fortunately, the lack of any one of these abilities should not prove discouraging, since the means for improvement are available to us. Suppose we do not recognise faces easily?

For instance, a lady whom we have seen or to whom we have spoken on one occasion may seem a complete stranger when we see her again wearing a different dress or, in contrast to our first meeting, with or without a hat. In such a case, what are we to do to improve our memory?

How to Remember Faces

If we wish to recognise a person when we meet him again, we must be able to form a mental image of him and by so doing bring his face accurately before our mind's eye whenever we choose. The easiest way to do this would be to make a drawing of his face. But most of us cannot draw a face accurately; and for the few who can, it is unnecessary, for an individual talented in drawing faces naturally has a good memory for them.

If it is necessary, therefore, to find a substitute for the drawings, the next best thing is to write a description of the person's face, not merely limiting ourselves to the colour of his eyes and hair but giving, rather, a description which includes all possible details, such as the shape of his nose, mouth, and ears. The way he wears his hair, the shape of his shoulders, and his approximate weight and height should also be noted.

To those who have a keen faculty of observation this may seem easy, while for others who lack this faculty it may prove more difficult. These latter may be helped by taking the following steps:

(1) Observe a person with the express purpose of writing a detailed description of him.

(2) Choose a close friend or a relative you know very well.

(3) Do not allow too much time to elapse between meeting him and writing a description of him.

All three steps may be made gradually more difficult: (1) by choosing some person you remember having met at a time when you had no intention of writing a description of him; (2) by choosing for the purpose a mere nodding acquaintance or a person you have met only once; and (3) by allowing a longer period of time to elapse between meeting him and writing the description of him.

And now, what is to be done when we have finished our description? Surely our task is not yet completed.

Before taking the next step in this exercise for developing our memory for faces, it is important to note that thus far we have followed the line of procedure suggested for general memory training in Chapter III. This procedure may be summarised as follows: Look at a display of merchandise in a shop window, making a careful mental note of everything you observe. Leave the shop window and write down on a sheet of paper every object you saw in it.

Then return to the window and compare what you have written with the actual articles on display.

Finally, as I have emphasised, do not correct your written notes while you are making the comparison. Rather, impress upon your mind any errors you have made and correct them later at a distance from the window.

Accordingly, then, the next step in training the memory for faces is to make an effort to see again, and as soon as possible, the person selected for your practice, in order to compare him with the description you have written.

Just as in the matter of the shop window, it is not advisable, while in the presence of this person, to correct any mistakes you may have made. In fact, it is much better for our purposes to impress these mistakes upon your mind and make corrections later, when you are alone.

There are two important advantages to be gained by using this plan of writing descriptions and comparing them later. First, we are forced to pay more attention to a person's face if we plan to describe it later on.

Secondly, as a result of focusing conscious attention on people's faces, we begin to find ourselves studying them unconsciously and with no special effort—just as in the case of athletic games, which we are at first obliged to practise carefully and consciously but are later able to play automatically.

Time often spent in day-dreaming can be put to good use in this way: While riding in a bus or on a train, cultivate the habit of studying the face of some person sitting opposite you. Then, upon closing your eyes or looking away from him, make a mental description of his face. You can do this more easily if you pretend that a friend is anxious to meet this fellow-passenger at a certain place and that, never having seen him, the friend is relying upon you for a perfect description in order to recognise the person at sight.

In making a description remember never to include such things as suits or dresses, because apparel is often changed. Rather, confine your attention to face and stature, in short, to those characteristics which always remain the same.

Studying faces in public conveyances offers an excellent opportunity for comparing our mental pictures with the originals, since we have only to open our eyes and look at the person we have in mind.

A more difficult but also more instructive procedure is to compare several faces with one another. Over here, for instance, are brother and sister; and over there, parents and child. In what respect are their features similar, and in what ways do they differ? Which features of the child are like the mother's and which resemble those of the father, and so on?

Here, again, we must not be satisfied with the usual vague observation that there is "some similarity," but, on the contrary, we must go into as minute detail as we can.

Still better is the following exercise: Look through a biography or album which contains pictures of a person at different ages, observing in detail which of his features have changed through the years and which have not.

This exercise is extremely difficult, as such pictures are usually taken from different angles and, as a result, some present full-face poses and others show the face in right or left profile. But these differences make the task not only more difficult but also more effective.

Another method of remembering faces in general is the use of the principles of physiognomy. These are based upon the theory that the contour of the head and each feature of the face are indicative of a certain character trait. For instance:

A fat face	Love of comfort and ease
Forehead prominent at the brows and slanting back as it rises	Powers of quick decision
Forehead prominent at the top and flat at the brows	Slowness of decision
Long, protruding chin	Slowness of action

Deeply etched lines running up
and down between the eyebrows   Masterfulness

High-bridged nose   Argumentativeness

Deep-set eyes   Qualities of a good listener

In order to apply the principles of physiognomy as a means of developing memory, it is not necessary for us to *believe* in them. It will suffice if we assume the attitude of one who wishes to find out *whether* they are true. In order to decide, we must necessarily observe a face much more carefully than usual, and this close scrutiny will enable us to detect some outstanding features hitherto overlooked.

One thing is sure: If we have once studied a face according to the exacting rules of any theory of physiognomy, we shall not forget it for many years to come.

Of all the exercises given on the preceding pages, you may take your choice and practise those you like best. Each and every one of them will help to improve your memory for faces in general. Thus, you will be encouraged to apply your newly acquired ability when you meet a person whose face you particularly wish to remember.

How to Remember Names

To be able to recognise people's faces is not enough. Remembering their names is equally important. However, it is more difficult for most of us to recall the name of a new acquaintance than to remember his face. The reason is simple.

In Chapter III, I explained the distinction between eye-minded and ear-minded people. As you will remember, the former retain impressions received through the eye more readily, while the latter remember more clearly what they hear. About three-quarters of all human beings, it is known, are eye-minded, and only one-quarter are ear-minded. This is one reason why a face, being *seen*, is remembered more easily than a name, which is *heard*.

Another reason lies in the fact that in speaking to a person we look at him continually and thus establish a constant repetition of the visual image. On the other hand, his name is usually heard only once, and so the very important element of repetition is lacking.

There are, however, several rules which will help you to overcome these disadvantages. First, *get the name correctly*. We cannot remember a name if we fail to catch it, as is apt to occur if the new acquaintance is presented with a mumbled rather than a clearly pronounced introduction.

If the name has not been enunciated clearly and correctly, let us not hesitate to ask to have it repeated. No one will take offence at such a request, because it pleases people to know that you are deeply enough interested in them to want to be sure of their names.

After we have understood the name correctly, let us not merely say, "How do you do!" Rather, let us extend it to "How do you do, Mr. Palma," "Glad to know you, Mrs. Bartel," or the like. If possible, let us go a step farther and ask a question: "I knew a Mr. Palma in London. Do you know him?" Or, "Are you related to Mr. Bartel in Manchester?" These, or similar, questions are a considerable help in impressing the name on our minds.

Then let us use the name as soon and as often as possible in conversation with our new acquaintance, for repetition is always one of the foundation stones upon which memorising is built.

But most important of all is the necessity of giving

some thought to the new name. In order to do this effectively, we must bear the following vital facts in mind:

All names, no matter in what language they are, may be divided into two categories:

1. Names which have a meaning in themselves, such as Baker, Fisher, Salmon, Gold, Baer, Wood, Rose, Brown, Strong, Cooper, Smith and the like.

Also in this category belong those names which, while having in themselves no meaning, nevertheless serve to convey a meaning through a natural association of ideas. For instance, should your new acquaintance have a name such as Grant, Gillette, or Chrysler, it will bring to mind a well-known person, thus making it easier for you to remember it. Or the new name may be that of one of your friends; if it is, an association between the two is, of course, easily made.

2. Names which in themselves have no meaning. In such instances, it is necessary to substitute a word which comes as close as possible *in sound* to the name of the person whose name is to be remembered.

We are accustomed to finding such substitutes. In Chapter X, you will remember, we found substitutes for the names of the forty-one counties, and in Chapter XI we found substitutes for the names of the Sovereigns of England.

Whether we are trying to remember the name of the county of Cornwall or the name of a Mr. Cornwall makes no difference, since in both instances we can use as substitutes words given in Chapter X, such as corn, cornea, corner, cornet, cornflower, cornice, cornucopia, etc. It goes without saying that it is easier to remember a substitute word which has a meaning than a name having no meaning in itself. It remains only to decide, when the actual need arises, which of the many available words to choose as a substitute for a name that is difficult to remember.

ASSOCIATING THE PERSON WITH HIS NAME

The third and last step, therefore, is to form a mental link between the person and his name. This will not prove difficult for persons who are in the habit of forming associations. And it will be easy for those who have put into practice the exercises suggested in the preceding chapters, for, as they will discover, there is very little difference between the methods indicated in the foregoing chapter for making associations and those I shall now give for connecting a person's name with the person himself.

To relate an individual with his name, we may choose some aspect of his appearance, manner, business or profession, and so on. Naturally, the more we know about the person, the more easily we can make the association. This is because the connection itself, and also the choice of a substitute word, should it be necessary, depend mainly upon the characteristics of the person we have in mind.

Assuming that the use of a substitute word is necessary, I shall return to Mr. Cornwall, for whose name I should choose the following substitutes:

Corn, if Mr. Cornwall walks badly because he has corns.

Cornea, if his eyesight is particularly keen or particularly poor.

Corner, if he lives in a corner house.

Needless to say, we shall not have to use a substitute word if we can find some direct relation between Mr.

Cornwall and the county of Cornwall; if, for instance, he comes from Bodmin or Penzance; if he regularly spends his holidays in Cornwall; or, in fact, if there is any natural association of a similar kind.

To get away from the name of a county, let us suppose we meet a man whose name is Lyon. The name "Lyon" is a variant of *lion* and identical in sound. Therefore, we may use the animal so named as a substitute for the name of our new acquaintance.

We could do the same with such names as Leon, Leonard, or Lionel. Such an association is made more easily if the man has performed some heroic act during the war or in private life. And it is better still if he happens to be hardy and gallant in appearance.

By a sort of reverse process, our association is made just as readily if the man suggests the exact opposite in appearance, or if he bears a reputation for cowardice. We have previously found that an association of ideas may be based upon contrasts as well as similarities.

If this man has travelled extensively in foreign countries, it may prove helpful to picture him shooting a lion. In fact, countless possibilities will occur to us upon a little thought. However, if we cannot find a logical association, we must try to picture this man with a lion or in a lion's cage, for even completely illogical images, originating solely in our fancy, will help us to remember the name whenever we meet the person again.

If the new name lacks both a meaning in itself and the possibilities for a natural association of ideas, we shall have to substitute a word which resembles it as closely as possible *in sound*.

Suppose we are introduced to a Mr. Dalloway, whose name is pronounced with the accent on the first syllable. We may substitute any of the following words:

delegate, delicate, delicacy, Delaware, deluge, and so on. From among these words, all of which are similar in sound to "Dalloway," we shall choose for our substitute word the one that will be easiest to associate with him. For instance, if we met him at a conference to which he was a delegate, we would try to remember his name by associating it with the word *delegate*. If we met him at a dinner-party, the association *delicacy* might be better. Therefore, our choice would depend entirely on the man's personality, the circumstances under which we met him, in short, on everything connected in our minds with Mr. Dalloway.

PREPARING FOR FUTURE MEETINGS WITH A NEW ACQUAINTANCE

Each new person with whom we become acquainted affords us an opportunity for further exercises. All that is required of us is that we apply the rules given above to the persons we wish to remember. Suppose we were to meet the aforementioned Mr. Cornwall on a nice spring morning. Our procedure during the evening of the same day should be as follows: We try to draw an actual picture of Mr. Cornwall. Should this prove too difficult a task, we form a mental image of him, recalling his build, height, face, appearance, voice, and so forth as accurately as we can. In doing so, we should emphasise and even exaggerate the feature which seemed to us most noticeable as we looked at him. This will help us to recall the association we made between person and name, somewhat in this way: This morning I met the man whose picture I have just drawn in my mind. I determined never to forget his name.

He walked badly. Walking badly reminds me of corns . . . his name is Cornwall.

He told me that his eyesight was particularly keen (or particularly poor). Eyesight reminds me of cornea . . . his name is Cornwall.

The house in which he lived is on a corner . . . his name is Cornwall.

When we have formed these associations mentally, we must be sure to write down the name. Writing it down helps for several reasons. It obliges us to think of the spelling, which, in turn, helps us to concentrate more fully on the name. Also, we use our eyes while writing, and we have already learned how important visual impressions are for our memories.

After we have done all this, we can enjoy a good night's sleep and follow the same procedure on the next day. There are no general rules as to how often this should be done, since there is a considerable variation among individuals in functioning of memory. However, the following will prove a safe rule for all to heed: Repeat the procedure until you feel sure you will remember Mr. Cornwall's face and his name whenever and wherever you may happen to meet him again. Lyon expresses this thought very well by saying: "Here again we find that if one is unable to take a good snapshot, he must fall back upon the old reliable method of time exposure."

HOW TO REMEMBER MANY PEOPLE AT ONE TIME

For most people the real difficulty arises when they meet at one time, not one person, but a dozen or more, whether it be at a conference, a large business meeting, or a private party. Needless to say, the general rules given above are not to be changed but simply applied more vigorously, for, when we meet many new persons on a particular occasion, our attention has a tendency to become more divided than when we meet only one person.

Usually we find ourselves in an unfamiliar room. We are surrounded by many people, most of them strangers to us. Furthermore, a multitude of strange new impressions are forcing themselves upon us. Therefore our most important task is to prevent any diversion of our attention and to focus it under all circumstances on the person to whom we are being introduced, especially on his name. Here are the other rules:

1. Try to limit the number of strangers you will meet at one time by arriving early at the meeting or party. Those who attend will arrive one by one, or, at the most, by twos and threes, and you will find it much easier to impress twenty new names upon your mind if they are given at intervals of from twenty to thirty minutes than if you hear them all at once.

2. Prevent the person who introduces you from mumbling the names and pronouncing them too rapidly. You can do so in a polite way by repeating the name of each person to whom you are being introduced. "How do you do, Miss Neal!" "I am glad to meet you, Mr. Hindle!"

I have mentioned this method previously in connection with meeting a single person, but obviously it is still more important if you are introduced to many people at the same time. Repeating the name will give you the time needed for making your association and prevent the person who is making the introductions from giving the names faster than you can mentally assimilate them.

3. As soon as you can find an opportunity, look for a quiet spot and see whether you can remember the various associations you have made and whether, with

their aid, you can recall the names of the persons who are present.

If you find that the names of any persons have escaped you, get them again by asking either your host or somebody else who knows them. Repeat the same procedure as often as necessary in order to fix all the names in your mind.

These rules should not be difficult for persons accustomed to forming mental associations. Most of my students have confirmed the fact that this method works after a short period of training.

A feat performed by one of my students at a lecture I once gave surprised everyone in the audience except my own students. This lady asked about thirty people, who were strangers to her, to give her their names, real or fictitious, along with a short remark or phrase, true or false, which she might associate in her mind with the name, e.g., "My name is Dawson. I have just read a book called ————." After hearing them once only, she was able to repeat both names and remarks—and she had joined my class because she was dissatisfied with her memory!

At a dinner of the "Dr. Furst Memory Club" Mr. Samuel Ebenstein, a lawyer and chairman for the evening, repeated the exact first and second names of forty persons who were guests of club members and whom he had never met before they entered the ballroom of the hotel and were introduced to him as they entered.

To associate not only the name but also certain facts with the new acquaintance is a rule I always stress in my classes. How to do it will be discussed later on in this book.

Every good salesman knows how helpful it is to

know as much as he can about the family, health, and
hobbies of a customer. And even in social contacts,
such information proves definitely advantageous.

Dr. Wendell White makes the following statement in
his *Psychology in Living*: "Appreciation of another
person is often reflected in the information revealed
regarding him. Almost everyone is aware of this, and so
when an individual finds that things about him are
known and remembered he is highly complimented.
Realising this fact, many persons make it a point to
acquaint themselves with another person or his interests,
and to reveal such information with the purpose of
expressing appreciation of him in a circuitous way.
Perhaps it was *Pithecanthropus erectus* who first said,
and said with insight into human nature, that if you
mean to have another person think you appreciate his
worth you must know his name. The teacher who does
not learn the names of those under her instruction, the
foreman who refers to the workers with an expression
such as 'You there', and the professional man who
forgets the names of his clients, may find other means of
expressing appreciation quite ineffective. And everyone,
to make his respect for someone else felt and to have
influence, must reveal knowledge of one kind or another
in regard to that person. By observing things pertaining
to another person—things ranging from little artistic
effects whereby a woman makes herself more charming,
or makes the home more attractive, to great achievement—we make ourselves pleasant associates."

Unfortunately, just the opposite can be said of many
salespeople, regardless of how well trained they may
be in their respective fields. This is as true of assistants
behind the counter as of salesmen on the road. John D.
Rockefeller once said about travelling salesmen: "First,
I'm surprised at how little they know about me before

they come to see me; and, after I've seen them, I'm equally surprised at how little they know about the things they offer me."

Very often we can prepare ourselves in advance for an important meeting. For instance, the chairman of a conference usually knows beforehand the names of the delegates, or at least the greater part of them. Thus, a person who is interested in getting the names correctly may be able to obtain them through the chairman or his secretary.

We know that the process of remembering a person's name actually comprises three steps: remembering the face, remembering the name, and finally linking the face with the name. Knowing the names beforehand, then, will enable us to prepare the second step in advance—that is, familiarise ourselves with the names and think of various substitutes for them. In short, we can master this second step before the actual meeting and thereby reduce our task by about one-third.

A friend and I were once on our way to a conference where I was due to give a lecture. With the help of a list which my friend had I was able to memorise the names of the conference delegates, associating each with a fact about him which my friend kindly supplied. Later on, when one of the delegates was introduced to me, he was very much surprised to be asked how he liked the new offices into which his firm had recently moved. Another delegate was equally astonished when, on our being introduced, I asked him whether his small son had fully recovered from his recent illness.

And *you* could do the same. Prepare for each meeting you attend by making yourself familiar with the names of the persons who will be present. This will give you more help than will any other kind of preparation.

PREPARING FOR FUTURE MEETINGS WITH MANY PERSONS WE HAVE MET AT ONE TIME

It is important, after we have met many people at a party or other function, not to relax in our efforts. On the contrary, now is the very time to apply our general rules of memory training to the specific problem of making sure that we shall recognise all the people we have met when we see them again.

In order to do this, we shall have to recall every person we met on the particular occasion. The simplest way to do so is to follow a certain order. If we met these people at a private party, we should try to remember the order in which they were seated in relation to ourselves; or, if they were introduced to us at a conference or business meeting, the order in which the delegates or the representatives of the different business firms were seated.

In fact, any order is permissible if it enables us, beyond a doubt, to recall every person who was present. From this point we again follow the now familiar rules: try to draw a mental picture of each person, recalling his appearance, face, voice, and particularly the things we heard him say. We should recall, also, the associations we made in connection with him, and through them make sure that his name remains in our minds.

Never postpone this work to the following day. Do it immediately after the meeting, for that is the time when all impressions are still clear in our minds. A hunting dog will follow a fresh scent more readily than an old one.

Students in my classes, which consist of from thirty to fifty members, are invariably amazed when I call each by name at the second session. And this in spite of the fact that I seldom have the opportunity of meeting any of them personally before the first session.

No secret is involved. It is merely a matter of applying the rules which I have given above. I prepare for the first session by memorising carefully the names of those who have already enrolled, thus making it easier to form the desired association when they answer the roll-call in class.

Following the meeting, I study the names and recall the particular place where each sat. This procedure helps immensely, for even though the students are not apt to take the same places at the next session, it helps me to recall each person's appearance. I repeat this procedure before the second session and, having done so, I am fairly certain of recognising everyone.

Besides the opportunity for pleasant contacts with my students, each new class in this way affords an opportunity for training my own memory. For these two reasons I earnestly recommend this procedure to all presidents and chairmen whose responsibility it is to conduct large meetings; also to all business executives and anyone who desires to progress in his business or social life. The ability to recognise people is rightly called the first important rung on the ladder of success!

How to Remember First Names

As we all know, people are interested not only in their last names but also in their first, or Christian, names. If proof of this were needed, it is furnished by an interesting advertising campaign conducted by the Ethyl Corporation.

To point up in each advertisement the fact that "Ethyl" is a trade name, the firm offered gratis an attractive booklet entitled "What's in a Name." This booklet dealt with Christian names and revealed, for instance, that Charlotte means "strong and valiant";

Sylvia means "of the forest"; Harold means "leader of an army"; and Philip means "lover of horses."

Most interesting for our purpose is the fact that over two million copies of the booklet had been requested by the public within one year after publication. "There is no indication that the interest of the public is diminishing to any great extent," the Ethyl Corporation wrote in reply to a question I addressed to them about it.

Since we are convinced of the importance of remembering Christian names, we must find a way of recalling them. Obviously, this method cannot be the same as the one we use for surnames. However, I have three possibilities to offer:

1. You can use the correct meaning of the Christian name if you know the meaning or if you have the time and facilities for looking it up. In most cases, connecting this meaning with the person in question will suffice. For instance, if my friend Sylvia lives near a wood, or if I met her in the woods, the connection is easy. And the same holds true if Harold, whose name I wish to remember, happens to be an officer in the army or is on his way to a commission.

2. If you do not know the meaning of the name, you may try associating it with somebody else you know who has the same first name. Since everybody knows a hundred times as many people as there are common first names, such a connection usually causes little difficulty.

3. The third possibility is concerned with initials. Let us suppose you wish to keep in mind two initials instead of two Christian names, as is often the case in dealing with business acquaintances to whom you write more frequently than speak. In this instance, I suggest that you expand the initials into two adjectives starting with

the initials. They will give you a simple connection with the person in question or with his last name. I quote as examples the names of two of my students:

Mr. J. L. Warren   The substitute for **Warren** is **war.**
I think of a just but long war.

Mr. W. A. Ayres   The substitute for **Ayres** is **air.**
Think of wonderful autumn air.

Now you are in possession of all the ways for remembering surnames and first names. Try them out and let me know how they work and whether you have found any suggestions which may prove still more effective.

CHAPTER XIII

USING YOUR LIVING-ROOM AS A MEANS OF REMEMBERING WORDS

WITHOUT turning back, repeat the series beginning with the word **school** and ending with the word **book**. You can still repeat this series by heart, *provided you supplied your own association-laws at the time and did not restrict yourself to those I suggested.*

If you make an honest effort you will find that you can repeat the series backward, too; that is, begin with the word *book* and end with the word *school*.

In spite of this forward step, encouraging as it is, we still have one disadvantage to overcome in mastering our method, in fact any method. And this is: You can repeat this series forward or backward, but you cannot possibly name the fifth or eighth word in the series. Of course we can search out these words by starting at the beginning and counting them off. But we want to try to avoid this counting off and tell immediately which word belongs to any number at all. How can this be done?

There are things so familiarly connected in our minds with figures that counting off no longer comes into question. To these belong, for instance, the names of the twelve months. Every child knows that April is the fourth month, August the eighth, and December the twelfth month of the year without having to start with January and count off to four or eight or twelve.

127

Therefore we might tie up the words which we want to remember in their serial order with the names of the months, and by so doing we would have made a good start. In itself this method is plausible, but it has a drawback in the fact that the names of the months are themselves abstract. And association with abstract ideas is, as we know from experience, more difficult than association with concrete things.

The easiest way to demonstrate visual and concrete association is to make use of the room in which you are reading this book. Look around and select the ten most striking objects that meet your eye. Number them in the sequence in which you see them, beginning at your left and proceeding clockwise to your right. Suppose that your room is furnished like the one in the following illustration.

You might choose the following objects:

1. Radio
2. Chair
3. Window
4. Lamp
5. Desk

6. Safe
7. Flag
8. Money-box
9. Picture (showing people)
10. Map

The objects numbered from 1 to 5 are on the left side of the room; those numbered from 6 to 10 are on the right.

Don't try to memorise this drawing. You will be wasting effort if you do. But keep it before you while you do the exercise outlined in this chapter. After all, you have the alternative of doing the exercise with the furniture in your own room, which is before your very eyes. Even with your eyes closed you could visualise your own room, especially the ten objects which you have selected for the purpose of your study.

1. RADIO 2. CHAIR 3. WINDOW 4. LAMP 5. DESK 6. SAFE 7. FLAG 8. MONEY-BOX 9. PICTURE 10. MAP

Now let us try to learn a series of ten words with the help of this furniture. These ten words are:

1. Speech   2. Arms   3. House   4. Search   5. Property
6. Criminal 7. Jury   8. Bail   9. People   10. State

Furthermore, let us try to memorise these words by connecting them with the objects we numbered above:

1. Object number 1 is **radio**. The word to remember is **speech**. Since we are accustomed to hear many speeches over the radio, there is no difficulty in connecting these two items in our minds.

2. Object number 2 is **chair.** The word to remember is **arms.** I suggest that you use armchair as a link between chair and arms. Thus, chair will recall to your mind an armchair and consequently arms.

3. The third object is **window**. The word to remember is **house**. A window is an important part of a house because it provides ventilation.

4. The fourth object is **lamp**. The word to remember is **search**. The association is easy if we think of a searchlight.

5. The fifth object is **desk.** The word to remember is **property.** Connection: my desk is the most important piece of personal property in my office.

6. The sixth object is **safe**. The word to remember is **criminal**. Connection: the thing most coveted by a criminal is a safe containing money and valuables.

7. The seventh object is the **flag.** The word to remember is **jury**. To serve the flag is a duty; so, too, is serving on a jury.

8. The eighth object is **money-box.** The word to remember is **bail**. Connection: a man under arrest generally uses his savings for bail.

9. The ninth object is **picture**. The word to remember is **people.** We can make the connection easily if we look at the people in the picture.

10. The tenth object is a **map,** which gives us an easy connection with **state** as the word which is to be remembered.

Now if you will look again at the sketch and run through the numbered pieces of furniture once more, you will find that as a result of the proposed associations you can immediately recall each word in the series you just learned.

You will find that this method made it very easy for you to learn the following list of fictional titles. As a matter of fact, the words which I chose are the key words of each title. The list reads:

1. *Freedom of Speech*
2. *Up in Arms*
3. *A House of Cards*
4. *In Search of Security*
5. *A Man of Property*
6. *Death of a Criminal*
7. *Trial by Jury*
8. *Released on Bail*
9. *People of Importance*
10. *An Affair of State*

The advantage of such a method of association—and I shall discuss its disadvantages shortly—consists in the fact that it is impossible to confuse the order of the titles as long as we keep the numbers of the pieces of furniture in our minds or before our eyes. If I know that number 5 is **desk,** I must also know that **property** is the fifth thought, since I am conscious of the association between desk and property.

If you compare the method used in Chapter VII in learning Winston Churchill's speech with the method applied to learning the contents of the above list, the following difference will immediately be evident:

We learned the list by associating each title in it with

the furniture of a room. The underlying principle is that we peg, or hook, each item to something already in our minds before we even know the new words we are to learn. In the matter of Winston Churchill's speech, however, we connected one thought with another thought without using any such prepared pegs, or hooks. Quite naturally you may ask, in the light of your study of this chapter, why we did not proceed in the same manner heretofore. Why did we not associate the first thought of the speech with our number 1 object, the second thought with our number 2 object, and so forth? Let me answer you in detail, for a clear understanding of this point is very important.

The difference between the two methods can best be illustrated by the following diagram:

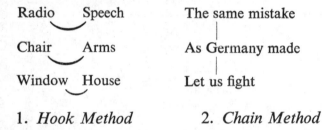

Radio ⌣ Speech	The same mistake
Chair ⌣ Arms	As Germany made
Window ⌣ House	Let us fight

1. *Hook Method*   2. *Chain Method*

In the first method, the items to be remembered are hung on given pegs, or hooks. Therefore this is called the "hook method."

In the second method, the items to be remembered are strung out one after the other and connected as in a chain. Therefore this is called the "chain method". For practical use it is especially important for you to determine which of these two methods is easier, more practicable, and more likely to retain facts in your memory for a long period of time.

When I bring up this question in my memory classes, the students are usually divided in opinion—some of them vote for the first method and others for the second method. When a question elicits two widely different responses, one may safely conclude that the true answer lies somewhere in between. Or it may be that the determining factor is a point of view as yet unknown. Indeed, in this instance it is just that as yet unknown point of view which is the determinant. Namely, the answer to this question depends upon still another question, which involves the nature of the things to be remembered.

This question is: are the items to be remembered related to each other, or unrelated? In the case of Winston Churchill's address or any other speech, there is such a relationship between the various thoughts embodied in the speech. Whenever such a logical relationship exists, it would surely be a mistake, and also make our task of remembering more difficult, if we deliberately tore this relationship apart in order to create another relationship. It is much easier for us to preserve a relationship which already exists and to make use of it than to create new associations with pieces of furniture or other objects which are outside the chain of thought we are trying to develop.

The exact opposite holds true for the list of titles. In this case there is no logical association between the separate items. *Up in Arms* (number 2) has no relationship to *A House of Cards* (number 3). Furthermore, it is desirable and sometimes necessary—for instance, in examinations—to know the numbers of the items, too. Only the hook method can supply this advantage. The chain method cannot.

If we assemble all these facts and hold tight to the main idea—that the chain method is to be used when a logical association already exists—we find that its principal use lies in memorising speeches, regardless of whether the speech is original or merely quoted; in committing newspaper articles to memory; in remembering the tables of contents of books; in short, in recalling anything that has a logical relationship within itself. If you wish to apply the chain method to memorising a speech which you have composed yourself, I call your attention specifically to Part Two of this book, "The Art of Public Address."

On the contrary, the hook method should always be used when a definite series of ideas is involved and it is necessary to know, in addition, every single word or object outside the sequence or series.

I shall later discuss the field of its chief application, namely the separate hours of the day in a complete daily time-table of living.

But I do not want to leave the discussion of the intrinsic differences between these two methods without emphasising the following: Impressing a chosen matter in your mind by the chain method usually takes longer than by the hook method.

On the other hand, the chain method has the advantage of impressing a matter for a considerably longer period of remembrance. The things that I have impressed on my mind by a chain remain with me all the time, or at least for many years.

In the case of the hook method, however, we must remember that the single hooks are used again and again for other matters, so that they are not very well suited for memory over a long period of time. But both methods have the common advantage of training the memory by requiring associations. Whichever method we use, every experience in it teaches us whether or not our power of concentration has relaxed. When it relaxes, we later notice that the association in question was missing. We can therefore determine our power of concentration with almost mathematical exactitude. How important such training is, has been acknowledged by various authorities in the field of memory training.

For example, in discussing "Using Your Memory" two teachers of public speaking, Dwight E. Watkins and Herbert F. de Bower, write: "Those things are impressive which stimulate the senses and mental activity most deeply. Therefore, in order to impress anything upon the mind so that it will be remembered, it is necessary often to *sharpen its impact* upon the mind. This means that we must *observe closely*, and memory, therefore, is largely a matter of attention and concentration.

"Most speakers learn to cultivate these abilities by mere force of necessity and they discover for themselves various methods that will enable them to 'get along.' They often overlook, however, the psychological law which is of perhaps the greatest value in relation to the memory, viz. the *law of association*. We remember best those things that we associate with things that we already know and have 'at our finger-tips'."

Again, in his book *Practical Psychology* Dr. Henry Knight Miller counsels: "Make clear and deep impressions. The clarity and depth will depend on the degree of attention and concentration. Fasten your attention on the thing you wish to remember. . . . Associate the thing you want to remember with something else. . . . In recalling make the association. Take a mental fishing-line, bait the hook with the association and throw it down into the depths of the subconscious until it catches."

In my memory classes many of the students assure me, time and again, that this kind of training heightens their ability to concentrate and to memorise facts for everyday use, whether professional or personal.

The principal advantage in the hook method lies in the fact that it makes us memory-conscious; that is, we become conscious of how many things in life depend upon our ability to make our memories function correctly, and of how we can make the poorest memory a good one and a normal memory an exceptional one.

Yet limiting the hook method to the pieces of furniture in our room has certain grave weaknesses which we must try to overcome in some way. The most serious weakness is the fact that the pieces of furniture are limited in number. Of course, we could extend the number; but if we do so, we run the risk of getting mixed up or of making mistakes. Indeed, the very fact that we can get mixed up is the second weakness in the method. For instance, if the objects in the drawing were not numbered, we should have no definite way of knowing whether the desk is number 4 or number 5. Therefore we must try to correct these weaknesses simultaneously. In order to do so, we shall use a numerical code as outlined in the next chapters.

CHAPTER XIV

NUMERICAL CODES

MOST people find it extremely difficult to remember figures, although it is necessary to do so in every phase of modern life. Not only in school and college but in everyday life a great deal of time is spent in the tedious task of impressing abstract numbers on our memories.

The thought of our school-days brings back a haze of figures learned through painful repetition, historical dates, the height of mountains, the population statistics of cities and countries, and usually a great number of mathematical and chemical formulas as well, which consist largely of numbers.

The memorising of numbers in one form or another is essential for the student, whatever profession or trade he plans to follow. The young lawyer must memorise the numbered paragraphs in volumes on law or the dates of important legal decisions. The doctor has to master, practically verbatim, countless formulas, however wearisome the task may seem.

For the business man and the merchant figures play an equally important role. Cost and selling price, the telephone numbers of business acquaintances, figures in an infinite variety of forms must burden the minds of all of us.

The chief difficulty in memorising numbers is due to the fact that they are abstract. Not even the liveliest imagination can succeed in making a mental picture of them. Take, for instance, the number 70. We can imagine an old man of seventy, or picture a seventieth anniversary jubilee, and the like, but the abstract number 70, without reference to some concrete matter, is beyond our imagination.

We can overcome this lack of imagination, however, by applying mnemotechnics and translating figures in a simple, apt fashion into words, so that there is no further difficulty in remembering them. The method is simplicity itself—the substitution of letters for figures in such a way that the letters have an easy connection with the figures.

The substitution of letters for figures is, of course, a practice familiar to all readers who understand merchandising. The merchant often likes to have the cost price of a piece of goods on the price tag without its being so evident that the customer can figure out the profit. For this purpose he does not use unrelated letters in making his code but only those which form words and are therefore comparatively easy to remember.

For instance, he may select the words "pounds" and "pence," writing the word "pounds" as "pouds" and the word "pence" as "encx", since he cannot repeat a letter in the code.´ The substitution of figures would therefore be:

P O U D S & E N C X
1 2 3 4 5 6 7 8 9 0

A piece of goods whose cost price was £3.86 would therefore be labelled U/N&. The merchant himself would be able to read the tag as £3.86, while the customer, ignorant of the key, would not be able to translate the code into figures. Theoretically, there is no reason why we should not adopt these words with their code for mnemotechnics. In practice, however, a different system has been developed, a system based on the frequency with which letters recur in the English language, completely disregarding the vowels.

This numerical system has been used by Berol, Roth, Loisette and other writers on the subject, and it seems pointless not to avail ourselves of a tested method which has proved satisfactory for many years.

In forming our numerical code, the following substitution of letters for numerals is the one usually adopted:

1 is indicated by the letter *t*, because the *t* has 1 downstroke.

2 by *n* because *n* has 2 downstrokes.

3 by *m* because *m* has 3 downstrokes.

4 by *r* because the word "four" has four letters of which *r* is the fourth; and besides, *r* is the emphatic consonant in the word "four."

5 by l because Roman capital *L* means 50.

6 by *J*. If you turn 6 round you practically have *J*.

7 by *K*. The initial stroke in writing a calligraphic *K* is similar to a 7.

8 by *f*. The small written *f* and the number 8 both have two loops.

9 by p. If you turn 9 round, you have *P*.

0 by *z*, because *z* is the last letter in the alphabet, and the familiar word *zero*, which means nought, begins with *z*.

As you see from reading this code system, it is extremely simple to understand and use. We now have the following:

1 2 3 4 5 6 7 8 9 0
t n m r l j k f p z

Once the principle of substitution is clear, the next step is to extend its application. In doing this, it must be borne in mind that in this method no attention is paid to spelling; it is based entirely on the *sound* of the letters. Consequently, all letters which sound alike are considered, for our purposes, identical, and we can therefore extend the above substitutions as follows:

For the cipher 1: Use *d* or *th*, as well as *t*, since all three are similar in sound.

For the cipher 6: Similar to the sound of *j* are the sounds of *ch* and *sh*, as, for instance, in the words *chair* and *ship*. In addition, *g* when it has a soft sound as in *George*, *germ*, or *giant*.

For the cipher 7: Hard *g* belongs with the *k* sound, because in such words as *garden*, *game*, *guest*, the sound is similar. In this group, also, belongs the hard *c*, as in *calm*, *call*, *Cambridge*.

For the cipher 8: Similar to the sound of *f* is the consonant *v*, and also *ph* in such words as *phantasm*, *phone*, *phase*.

For the cipher 9: *p* sounds like *b*, for it also is a labial.

For the cipher 0: *z* is phonetically like *s*, as is also soft *c*, in such words as *cipher*, *civic*, *cigar*.

This completes the system of numerals and gives us the following:

1	2	3	4	5	6	7	8	9	0
t	*n*	*m*	*r*	*l*	*j*	*k*	*f*	*p*	*z*
d					*sh*	hard *g*	*v*	*b*	*s*
th					*ch*	hard *c*	*ph*		soft *c*
					soft *g*	*ng*			
					tch, dg	*q*			

In order to prevent any misunderstanding, let me emphasise the following points:

(1) Vowels and the consonants *w* and *h* have no numerical values, when they stand alone. This is not true when *h* is used in conjunction with another consonant to form a single sound. In this case the sound is the determinant. For instance, in accordance with the foregoing rules of substitution, *enough* would be expressed by the figures 28, because the consonants *gh* in this instance are sounded as *f*.

(2) Consonants not listed in the above table, but with sounds similar to those given, are, of course, to be classified in like manner. For example, *q* has the numerical value of 7, because it sounds like *k*. *X* is rated, as a rule, as 70 because it sounds like *ks* in such words as *extra* and *extract*. However, when it is pronounced like *z*, as in *xylophone*, it is valued as 0.

(3) Double consonants count as single ones, since the sound of a double consonant is identical with that of a single consonant. For instance, in the number code *letter* is considered as though spelled with one *t*.

(4) The phonic *ng* is coded as 7, like the hard sound of *g*, since it might easily be confused with *nk*, which is represented as two single consonants, 27.

(5) Since numbers that begin with 0 are rarely encountered outside mathematics, words beginning with *s* or *z* may be treated as though these two consonants did not exist. This rule, however, should be followed only for practical convenience and should never be used by readers who work with figures starting with 0.

All these rules are simple when one realises that sound —that is, the pronunciation of the word and not its written appearance—is the essential factor. For this reason the beginner is urged to begin by coding words he hears and not those he sees in print.

Here are some examples, with codes that are simple and present no difficulties:

9 1			14	
bet	= 91		dry	= 14
7 3			4 2	
game	= 73		iron	= 42
5 1 2			84 01	
litany	= 512		frost	= 8401
7 42 5			4 9 95 7	
kernel	= 7425		republic	= 49957

With a little practice it is easy to master this numerical code. In fact, it can be learned in about an hour. The best method is to go into your room or for a walk and ask yourself the numerical value of the various items that catch your eye.

For instance, if you see a book, you will know that "book" is 97. If you see a tree, you will know that "tree" is 14. If you see a river, your mind translates it into 484. It is far simpler than it appears at first sight.

The following words may be difficult for a beginner. But if you learn the basic rule—to follow the *sound* and not the appearance of the word—your difficulties will vanish.

Hello is 5, since the initial letter *h* has no code cipher and the double *l* is treated as single *l*.

Warrant is 421, since the *w* has no code cipher and double *r* is counted as 4.

Window is 21, since neither the initial nor the final *w* has any value.

Wing is 7: *w* is not counted, and *ng* is treated as *g*.

Warship is 469: *w* is not counted, and *sh*, a compound consonant, counts as 6.

Heart is 41: *h* is not counted.

Knack is 27: the initial *k* is silent and *ck* has the same sound as *k*.

Lamb is 53: the *b* is silent.

The *sound* alone is important in this numerical code. This can be demonstrated most clearly by words in which *gh* has different sounds:

Ghost is 701, because *gh* is pronounced like hard *g*.
Enough is 28, because *gh* is pronounced like *f*.
Neighbour is 294, because *gh* is entirely silent.

In the beginning, do not bother too much about the words which you have difficulty in coding. As you become more adept, you will find even the most difficult words rather easy to code. But do not make the mistake of attempting too soon to reverse the process and translate numbers into words. Although this is our final objective, our immediate concern is to learn to translate words into numbers. This is absolutely necessary.

Do not go on to the next section until you have mastered this numerical system so thoroughly that you can rapidly translate into the numerical code any object you observe. The efforts required of you are slight and as you go on you will find that they are well repaid.

CHAPTER XV

THE PRACTICAL APPLICATION OF NUMERICAL CODES

I ASSUME that before continuing you will have memorised the numerical code so well that you can substitute numbers for every word you hear or read. But we must remember we did not learn the numerical code in order to express words in numbers, but for the reverse purpose: to remember numbers through words. Everything that has been done up to this point was with this goal in mind.

Taking any word haphazardly, there is only one number-equivalent which is just right. On the other hand, there is a great variety of words which you can translate into this number. This is, as you see at a glance, of extraordinary advantage. It is also the reason why we left the various vowels and the consonants *w* and *h* without any number-value.

Take, for instance, the number 914. You can translate this into the words *poetry, battery, potter, patter, powder, better, betray, boudoir, butter*, etc. The flexibility of this method is naturally advantageous because of the large number of words which can be so simply formulated for practical purposes.

In everyday life you never note a number for itself alone, that is, without its connection with a fact, a subject or an event. If an event in history is concerned, it means the number belongs to a certain historical occurrence. If a geographical fact is concerned, the number is to be remembered in connection with the height of a mountain, the length of a river, the population of a town, or the like. If a telephone number, it is in connection with the person whose phone number it is. In every instance, therefore, the number is associated with something else and is meaningless when dissociated from it.

If you had a definite code word for each number, it would sometimes be difficult to establish a connection between the word and the event. Through careful practice you have now attained such facility in making associations that this difficulty should appear very slight. Nevertheless we must not forget that mnemotechny exists to make learning as simple as possible.

If we are not restricted to one word alone, if we have a choice among a great variety of words, it is naturally much easier to pick out *the* word with which the number is associated which best fits the fact, event or subject.

In order to make this task easier, I have prepared a little dictionary of numbers, to spare you the trouble of hunting through the big dictionary yourself for a suitable word or digging it up from memory.

So we proceed as follows: Assume you want to remember, or want your students to remember, the year 1914 as the beginning of the first World War. First we cross off the initial 1. We can always omit the thousands in historical figures without any danger, since we are not apt to be 1000 years wrong on an historical fact. Striking off the 1 simplifies our task.

For the number 914 the dictionary gives all the words I mentioned earlier and a few more, which we will talk about shortly. From these words we choose, say "battery," since this concept is very easy to tie up with "war." It is easier for a student to associate the word "battery" with war than to learn the number 1914 by heart. The two concepts—the word "battery" and the number "914"—mean the same to one who knows the numerical code.

Instead of "battery" you may choose "poetry" if you remember how many so-called poems of heroism were written by patriots at the beginning of the Great War.

Note that the actual word you choose is a matter of no importance and that you can choose one to suit your individual taste. *This fact shows the superiority of this flexible system which allows the arbitrary insertion of vowels.*

And after you see what great advantages a choice among various words offers in remembering figures, I will give you another method, likewise referring to the dictionary, which expands this choice considerably: *Practical usage has demonstrated that there is no point in translating more than three consonants of a word*, naturally the first three, in order to avoid errors. The other consonants we will completely disregard and by so doing we shall enhance considerably the number of words at our disposal.

If we stay with the number 914, besides the words already named, we can use "butterfly," because only the first three consonants are counted and the following consonants *f* and *l* are disregarded. Or we can use the following words to indicate 914: patriot, patron, paternoster, bedroom, buttermilk, petrifaction, petroleum, putrid, putter, putrescence.

This list does not exhaust the possibilities, but it shows this method offers such a variety of words that we always have the possibility of finding one which fits the case especially well. With this in mind, if we are to remember the year 1914 as the beginning of the first World War, we would presumably prefer the word "patriot" to all the others.

I will try now to present a variety of examples which will show you how this method operates in actual life.

History:

Battle of Agincourt, 1415—**artillery** (artillery-battle)

Congress of Vienna, 1815—**fatal** (the results of the congress were fatal for all concerned)

Magna Carta, 1215—**intellect** (the signing of the Magna Carta was a sign of awakening intelligence)

Newton discovered gravitation, 1656—**geology** (the magnetic qualities of the earth rest on geologic premises)

Geography:

The height of Niagara Falls is 571 feet—**liquid**
^{5 7 1}

The area of France is 212,659 square miles—
^{2 1 26 5 9}
No town shall bow

Chemistry:

Gold melts at 1945° F.—**pearl** (pearls—valuable—gold)

Silver melts at 1760° F.—**cashes** (cash—money—silver)

Water boils at 212° F.—**intense**.

Weight of water per cubic foot is 62·5 lbs.—**channel**.

Weight of sea water per cubic foot is 64 lbs.—**shore**.

Weight of cast iron per cubic foot is 450 lbs.—**rails**.

Instead of noting the first three consonants of a word, you can form complete sentences and count only the initial consonant of each word. There is a greater possibility of variation in this method and therefore it is easier to apply.

History:

Fugitive Slave Law 1850—**fugitive law sustained**.

Black Death reached England 1348—**medieval raging fever**.

Sir Isaac Newton died 1727—**gravity Newton's gravestone**.

Beethoven born 1770—**concerts crashing symphonies**.

Storming of the Bastille 1789—**caused free Paris**.

Beginning of Paris Peace Conference 1920—peace not stable.

Spanish Armada destroyed 1588—large fleet failed.

General examples:

Submarine cables first laid between England and France 1850—French language spoken.

The Amazon, the longest river, is 3,800 miles—most vast.

One cubic foot equals 1,728 cubic inches—the cubic number of feet.

Copper melts at 1,981° F.—twelve pennies form a dozen (copper suggests penny).

Lead melts at 621° F.—choose new type (in printing).

Now let us apply this method in memorising the reigns of the kings and queens of England. We have the choice of connecting the substituting word with the sovereign's name or with the substitute word which we gave in the list of sovereigns. It is more difficult to make our connection with the sovereign's name, as that presupposes some knowledge of the monarch himself. Therefore it is simpler to use the key word as a general rule, though in a few obvious instances, such as John, Mary, Elizabeth, Cromwell, etc., I have not followed that rule.

In the following example I give the linking words which seem simplest to me, and where it seems advisable I add substituting words for the date of accession. The sovereign series is repeated here for your convenience:

Wit wins Hester. Hens rely on John for ham, but Ed's enemy an emblem renounces. A hero's hell is huge. Heirs elect remember. Hectic in heaven etches Mary Elizabeth. Jades chat of Cromwell's chance in January at Wimbledon with Anne. Getting gen and gems, Germans were victors. Extra gelid is the effect of George on Elizabeth.

Now, in learning the dates, we must be careful to

select words which have a close connection with each sovereign or with the substituting words in the "story." Since it is taken for granted that anyone would know that the year of accession must start with 1, we need substituting words for the last three figures only. And as we need concern ourselves only with three figures in each case, it makes no difference how many consonants there are in the substituting words in addition to the initial three.

Here are the key words, with explanatory notes in case they are not clear:

1. William I	1066	witty	**judge**
2. William II	1087	winter	**fog**
3. Henry I	1100	head	**thesis** (brain work)
4. Stephen	1135	stir	**tumult** (civil war and struggle against Matilda)
5. Henry II	1154	hen	**dealer**
6. Richard I	1189	Lionheart	**tough boy**
7. John	1199		**white paper** (Magna Carta, 1215)
8. Henry III	1216	ham	**sandwich**
9. Edward I	1272	Ed	**nickname**
10. Edward II	1307	enemy	**massacre** (English massacred at Battle of Bannockburn, 1314)
11. Edward III	1327	emblem	**monogram**
12. Richard II	1377	renounce	**smoking**, or **my king** (forced to abdicate)
13. Henry IV	1399	hero	**imbibes**, or **my pope** (he was devoted to the Pope)
14. Henry V	1413	hell	**redeem** (he tried to redeem the territories lost to France)
15. Henry VI	1422	huge	**renown**
16. Edward IV	1461	heir (the h is silent)	**archduke**

17. Edward V	1483	elect	**are famous** (Edward V and his brother are famous as the Princes in the Tower)
18. Richard III	1483	remember	**war fame** (the famous Wars of the Roses ended with the Battle of Bosworth, 1485)
19. Henry VII	1485	hectic	**arrival**
20. Henry VIII	1509	heaven	**always happy**
21. Edward VI	1547	etch	**lyric** (he liked books and poetry)
22. Mary	1553		**well illuminated** (by the fires of Protestant bishops burned at the stake during Mary's reign)
23. Elizabeth	1558		**well loved, wily love,** or **all alive** (Elizabeth had "live" policy)
24. James I	1603	jade	**chessman** (chessman made of jade)
25. Charles I	1625	chat	**genial** (his death speech on the scaffold was genial)
26. Oliver Cromwell	1653		**shall aim,** or **Charles loses monarchy** (this is an example of how to use only the initial consonants as shown on pages 147-148)
27. Charles II	1660	Chancery	**judges**
28. James II	1685	January	**joyful**
29. William III and Mary	1689	Wimbledon	**chief hope**
30. Anne	1702		**cousin**
31. George I	1714	get	**gather**

32.	George II	1727	gentleman	**concord** (gentleman's agreement)
33.	George III	1760	gem	**catches** (the eye)
34.	George IV	1820	German	**offensive** (all the Georges were Germans from Hanover, German and offensive are easy to connect)
35.	William IV	1830	were	**famous** (famous for introducing civil marriages)
36.	Victoria	1837	victors	have **mocked**
37.	Edward VII	1901	extra	**postage**
38.	George V	1910	gelid	**baths**
39.	Edward VIII	1936	effect	**bombshell** (abdication had effect of bombshell)
40.	George VI	1936		**submission** (Germany and Japan submitted)
41.	Elizabeth II	1952		**splendour** (of Coronation)

All of these auxiliary key words have been chosen to be remembered after one or two readings. Thus you can learn the dates of the reigns in about one hour—a task which might take you several hours in the old-fashioned way of memorising.

CHAPTER XVI

THE BASIC SERIES OF KEY WORDS

THIS subject is one of the most important in the whole study of mnemotechny. As we stated at the end of Chapter XIII, a weakness of the hook method, as far as using furniture as hooks is concerned, is that the series goes only to 10 and we run the risk of getting mixed up if we try to extend it. I promised we could overcome this weakness by using the numerical code, and we will now proceed to do so.

If we have a series from 1 to 100 and if we know that the word *Europe* falls in this series, the word can be no other than 49. This is a simple combination for *r* and *p* and no error is possible. But although it is extremely easy to translate the word *Europe* into 49, it is not so simple a matter to remember that we chose *Europe* as the key word for the number 49. We might just as well have chosen another word that also means 49, for instance, Arab, harp, rap, rob, rub, or the like.

Now, how do we know which of these many available words was chosen as key word?

Almost all the published mnemotechnical systems have acknowledged the vast importance of a fixed system of key words for the numbers 1 to 100, but all suffer from this weakness: *100 words must be learned by heart for these numbers.*

Again and again the students in my classes have complained about this difficulty and therefore I have sought and finally found a method which corrects this weakness.

I have worked out a method whereby we have at our disposal an unalterable basic series of key words without the necessity of learning a single one of them by heart. Amazing things can be accomplished by this method once you have learned how to put it to work for you.

Our task in this connection is to find auxiliary words in such a manner that we know exactly which word *must* be used for each number without learning any word by heart.

For instance, if we have chosen the word cat for 71, we must be in a position to translate 71 into "cat" after months or years, and not into one of the many other words which the number might represent.

To reach this goal, we shall proceed by using the vowels in their usual order in the alphabet, a, e, i, o, u. In this serial order we insert the vowels between the consonants indicated by numbers until we have found a meaningful word.

If none of the vowels will give us a word (which is seldom the case), we use double vowels. With double vowels we try to follow an order which sounds fairly like a-e-i-o-u. With very few exceptions, this happens only with the numbers from 1 to 9.

But if we make it our goal to build a basic series of key words *which can be reconstructed by every reader without memorising*, something more is needed. Up to now it was advantageous for us to have several consonants at our disposal for each figure, for instance *t* and *d* and *th* for 1, or *k* and hard *g* and *ng* and hard *c* for 7. But with key words we must decide on one particular consonant, because it is otherwise impossible to recall the exact word in every instance. For this reason we make a definite selection from the available consonants:

We begin all the words from 10 to 19 with *t* (not with *d* or *th*)

from 60 to 69 with *ch* (except 66)

from 70 to 79 with hard *c*

from 80 to 89 with *f*

from 90 to 99 with *b*

I disregard the words from 20 to 59 at this point, since for the figures 2, 3, 4, and 5 only one consonant is given in the numerical code. There is therefore no choice in the matter. Here, too, we follow phonetics, and doubled letters count as one.

All this sounds theoretical and a bit complicated, and yet in essence it is very simple. Let us take the figures 30 to 39 as an example.

The figure 30 consists of the consonants *m* and *s*. If I insert an *a*, I have *mas*, or, since a double consonant is permissible, *mass*, a word which I can use since it is a noun.

The figure 31 consists of the consonants *m* and *t*. Inserting the first vowel, *a*, gives us the word *mat*, which again is a noun.

The figure 32 consists of the consonants *m* and *n*. Inserting the vowel *a* gives us the noun *man*.

The figure 33 consists of the consonants *m* and *m*. Inserting the vowel *a* gives us *mam*. For this I substitute *mama*, since the final *a* does not count.

In the same fashion I get:

34—mare

35—mail

36—match

When we come to 37, we can do nothing with the vowel *a*, since *mak* is not a word and *make* is not usually employed as a noun. Therefore I attempt to form a word with *e*, but *mek* too is not a word. With the insertion of *i* I get *mike*, which is so familiar a nickname for microphone that I can use it.

For figure 38, the insertion of the vowels *a*, *e*, *i*, and *o* forms no sensible word, so that I have to resort to *u*, and get *muff*.

Figure 39 is again simple, for inserting *a* between the consonants *m* and *p* gives me the word *map*.

In spite of this consistency in building up key words, certain exceptions and questions arise. For instance, one may waver between *light* and *lot* for 51. Theoretically, the vowel *i* precedes the vowel *o*, which indicates that *light* should be chosen.

On the other hand, the consonants *gh* in the word *light* might lead to mistakes, in spite of the fact that they are silent. For this reason I have chosen *lot*. For 53 one may hesitate between *lamb* and *lime*, since the *b* in *lamb* is silent. But because I have consistently tried to choose key words which have as few silent consonants as possible, I gave *lime* the preference. For the same reason I chose *cheque* instead of *chalk* for 67, and *cuff* instead of *calf* for 78.

The figure 66 is an unavoidable exception, since *j* must be used as the initial consonant and there is no suitable word beginning with *ch*.

By this method we build the following basic series of key words, a *series tremendously important for all mnemotechnical practice.*

I again emphasise the point that the reader who thoroughly understands how the words are constructed, *does not need to learn them by heart*, since he can *reconstruct* each word whenever occasion demands.

This series can be applied in many ways. First of all, with its help we can remember any other word series we choose, up to 100 words. I need merely refer to the method outlined in Chapter XIII.

SERIES OF KEY WORDS

1. tea	34. mare	67. cheque
2. Noah	35. mail	68. chaff
3. May	36. match	69. chap
4. ray	37. mike	70. case
5. law	38. muff	71. cat
6. Shaw (author)	39. map	72. can
7. key	40. race	73. cam
8. fee	41. rat	74. car
9. bay	42. rain	75. call
10. tease	43. ram	76. cash
11. tot	44. rear	77. cake
12. tan	45. rail	78. cuff
13. team	46. rash	79. cap
14. tar	47. rake	80. face
15. tale	48. reef	81. fate
16. touch	49. rap	82. fan
17. tack	50. lace	83. fame
18. toffee	51. lot	84. fare
19. tap	52. lane	85. fall
20. niece	53. lime	86. fish
21. net	54. lair	87. fake
22. noon	55. lull	88. fife
23. name	56. lash	89. fop
24. Nero	57. lake	90. base
25. nail	58. leaf	91. bat
26. niche	59. lap	92. ban
27. neck	60. chase	93. beam
28. nave	61. chat	94. bar
29. nap	62. chain	95. ball
30. mass	63. chime	96. batch
31. mat	64. chair	97. back
32. man	65. chill	98. beef
33. mama	66. judge	99. babe

The basic series of key words must gradually become so familiar that *word and number become identical* for the user. Once you have reached that point, you can easily learn not only any chosen series of words but figures as well.

When you have mastered the key words from 1 to 20, ask a friend to call out, one after the other, any twenty subjects he chooses. It is essential for your friend to write down the subjects beforehand, since you and he will otherwise lack a check list. When he calls the first subject on his list, tie it up with the first key word, or *tea*. Concentrate on this thought-association and do not let anything disturb you. When you have the connection clearly and firmly in mind, ask for the second subject. Connect it with the second key word, or *Noah*, and do not think back to the first.

Store up the twenty subjects in your memory in this way: as soon as the twenty have been called off, go over the key words in your thoughts. You will have no difficulty in associating the connections you previously set up. But your friend, who knows nothing of these thought processes, will be surprised and impressed at your ability to repeat the twenty subjects in proper order without a single mistake. And you can surprise him even more if you offer to call them out at random, instead of sequentially.

For instance, if he wants to know the tenth word, you will naturally not have to begin counting from the beginning. Since you know that number 10 is *tease*, you will be able to name the correct subject at once through the concept you have associated with it.

After you have made this experiment a few times, try it out in company. This is always an effective experiment and it will not only prove entertaining, but also reward you for the time and effort you spent in learning the series of key words.

But, of course, applause is not the real goal of the experiment. Our goal is twofold:

1. To exercise not only your imagination, but also your powers of concentration to a degree hitherto unknown. You will notice how quickly your imagination is developing, when you observe that the association of seemingly unrelated things steadily grows easier. You give your powers of concentration practice in that you really fix your undivided attention on the two subjects under consideration, for, if you do not, the connection is not made strong enough for you to recall it later.

2. To apply this thought series in everyday life. I have already given you some illustrations proving the practical advantages of this system, and I shall present additional examples before we approach the end of this chapter.

But first let us try to recall a series of numbers instead of words. Assume that you are to remember the following ten numbers consecutively:

57
86
74
65
60
15
62
76
52
33

The first word in our series of key words is *tea*. The number 57 is to be associated with it. For this number we substitute the key word for 57, or *lake*. Therefore we imagine someone sitting by a lake drinking tea. In this connection it is important to concentrate on the picture for a few seconds and not let it be a mere passing idea.

The second word of our series of key words is *Noah*.

The second number to be remembered in the list given above is 86. For this number we substitute the word *fish* from our series of key words, and therefore we must associate Noah with fish. The association is simple—we imagine Noah catching a fish.

The third word in the series of key words is *May*. The third number to be remembered is 74, *car* in the series. As an association I suggest we picture a drive in a new *car* on a fine *May* morning. In doing so you need not fear confusing the month of May with another month. You must not forget that *May* is the only month in the series of key words.

So confusion is impossible, even apart from the fact that in forming your association your starting point is not *car* but the key word *May*. If we proceed in this fashion we get the following connections, for which I add possible associations. These associations are, of course, not binding, for the reader should try to find associations which are better and more pertinent for him individually:

1. tea	—lake	(57) A man sits by a lake drinking tea.
2. Noah	—fish	(86) Noah catches a fish.
3. May	—car	(74) We drive in a new car on a May morning.
4. ray	—chill	(65) The chill was dispelled by the rays of the sun.
5. law	—chase	(60) The policeman chases the law-breaker.
6. Shaw	—tale	(15) Shaw wrote tales as well as plays and essays.
7. key	—chain	(62) The key hung on a chain.
8. fee	—cash	(76) Fees are paid in cash.
9. bay	—lane	(52) The bay is at the end of the lane.
10. tease	—mama	(33) Mama teases her child, or the child teases his mama.

If you proceed in this way it is not hard to remember a series of 100 numbers of 2 digits. Of course, you should not and must not attempt this time-consuming task all at once; restrict yourself to 20 or 30 numbers for a start. Practice of this sort, which should not take more than 15 or 20 minutes, is an *extraordinarily good exercise in concentration*. It forces the student to think *definitely*, therefore really to *concentrate* on the key word and its associated word.

Even momentary lack of attention finds its revenge: the attempt to recall the connected word fails, because the association was not impressed deeply enough on the mind. But if you repeat, without errors, some 20 or 30 numbers, you may be sure *you have improved your powers of concentration and therefore your memory considerably*.

One more word about the objections which have been raised against the series of key words. Occasionally it is asserted that numerical codes, a series of key words, etc., impose too great a task on our thinking apparatus and are too time-consuming in application. To this charge we can reply that all these may easily be acquired in 8 or 10 hours, and that this time is negligible when compared with the facility and ease we attain in remembering. *Shorthand offers the best analogy*. In learning it, the student must first of all memorise characters and outlines, but after that shorthand is a time-saver for everything that must be written down. In the same way, *mnemotechny is an aid to everything that must be kept in mind*.

CHAPTER XVII

YOUR DAILY TIME-TABLE

AMONG the hundreds of uses to which the basic series of key words may be put is its employment in adhering to a time-table for a specific day.

Let us suppose that you start your day at eight o'clock in the morning and that you have the following things to do, each of them at a specified hour:

8 A.M.	You have to pay your rent.
9 A.M.	You must get train reservations.
10 A.M.	You intend to wire congratulations to a bride and groom.
11 A.M.	You plan to enrol for a memory course.
12 NOON	You intend to buy a new radio.
1 P.M.	You have an engagement at the China Exhibition.
2 P.M.	You have a date for a boat ride.
3 P.M.	You want to order a bouquet for your wife.
4 P.M.	You have an appointment at your doctor's surgery.
5 P.M.	You must appear in court for a traffic violation.
6 P.M.	You have to look up an item in the public library.
7 P.M.	You have an appointment to look at a new flat.

Let us try to remember these engagements with the help of our basic list. Since the time-table starts at eight o'clock, we cannot start with number 1 (tea) as usual. We must start with number 8 (fee) because this is the only way to connect the time-table with the proper hour. The associations which I suggest for the time-table outlined above are as follows:

8 A.M.   Associate *fee* and *payment*. A fee is something you

pay out, and the word "payment" will bring the payment of rent to your mind.

9 A.M.   The ninth word of the basic list is *bay*. Form the connection: bay—steamer—*train*.

10 A.M.   The tenth word of the basic list is *tease*. Send a *congratulatory wire* to the newlyweds, but do not tease them.

11 A.M.   The word is *tot*. Connection: A *memory course* is helpful to tots and adults alike.

12 NOON   *Tan*. Connection: Visualise a tan *radio* set!

1 P.M.   (Now you have a choice of going back to number 1 or following Army and Navy time and continuing with 13. I have chosen the first alternative for the following examples.)

Number 1 is *tea*. The connection with the *China Exhibition* is easy if we think of the fact that tea comes from China or that we drink tea from china cups.

2 P.M.   *Noah*. Like Noah, you take a *ride on the water*.

3 P.M.   *May*. In May you see the nicest *flowers*.

4 P.M.   *Ray*. Think of your *physician* using X-rays to examine your body.

5 P.M.   *Law*. You have to appear in *court* because you violated a traffic law.

6 P.M.   *Shaw*. Connection: Shaw—author—book—*library*.

7 P.M.   *Key*. When you rent a new *flat*, see to it that you get the key.

Now try to recall these twelve scheduled appointments with the help of these associations. You should be able not only to repeat them in sequence, but also to know exactly what you had in mind to do at ten o'clock, four o'clock, seven o'clock, and so on.

Make up your mind not to use notes in the future, but to train your memory by using associations like those given above. If you do so, you will reap the advantage of being able to recall easily whatever you have to do during the day. Besides, if you do not write your appointments down on a slip of paper, you won't run the risk of losing the slip.

On completing her course, one of my students gave a brilliant demonstration of the success of this method before a large audience.

The audience called out arbitrary things for her to remember to do, which were also out of sequence, at specific hours of the day. All of the engagements, which extended over several days and which another one of my students wrote on a blackboard as the audience called them out, embraced not only appointments with a lawyer and a doctor but detailed business transactions.

After many things had been called out in no sequential order, the student was able to repeat the entire time-table without so much as a glance at the blackboard; that is, she named every single thing she was supposed to do at each specified hour.

At the conclusion of another course, the same sort of experiment was performed at another public gathering by students who went even further and repeated appointments through an entire week, naming the exact day and hour when the audience asked what the time was for a certain appointment; and naming the appointment, date, or errand when the audience asked what it was that was to be done on Wednesday at four o'clock, on Friday at eleven, or on Sunday at two o'clock.

I claim that the majority of my students are able to perform these feats of memory when they have finished the course. It is, of course, important that each of them apply this memory training to the field in which he is professionally active.

Another student of mine, a concert pianist and originator of a radio programme "Music of All Countries and

Races," often finds it desirable to announce the dates of birth and death of the composers whose music he is presenting. After having finished my course, he can remember the birth and death dates of more than three hundred composers, and he often amazes his audiences by mentioning them offhand when he is questioned about them.

CHAPTER XVIII

REMEMBERING NUMBERS WITH MORE THAN TWO DIGITS—TELEPHONE NUMBERS AND EXCHANGES

IF you have had trouble in mastering the system which I have outlined up to this point, you can skip this chapter. But if you find it easy to form associations and have practised it to some degree, you will find it worth while to learn this method of remembering larger numbers.

Let us begin, for the moment, with 4-digit numbers. The first question is: Will our basic series of key words meet the situation? Let us test it.

Assume the telephone number of my friend Smith is 4295. In our basic series of key words 42 is *rain* and 95 is *ball*. To remember the number I should picture my friend Smith playing ball in the rain.

After enough practice in forming associations, this picture will, unquestionably, recur to me when I try to recall Smith's phone number. But here we encounter a difficulty. Assume the telephone number is 9542 instead of 4295. We would form the same mental picture, for we could not form any other than that of Smith playing in the rain if we utilised the basic key words. The picture, then, can mean 4295 or 9542.

We must therefore find a corrective. For every word in the basic series of key words we write another, whatever immediately occurs to us. This word need not agree with the numerical code, since its place in the

165

series is determined by its close association with the respective basic key word.

If we begin with the first word in our basic series of key words and think of *tea*, most readers will think of *cup*, for the concept "a cup of tea" is a familiar one. But with many of the key words, the words that come to mind will vary with the individual, and will be different from those that occurred to me. That brings up an important rule: While it is desirable not to vary the words in the basic series of key words, it is not at all necessary to keep this secondary series unchanged.

Therefore, you may add to the basic key words whatever words occur to you in connection with them rather than merely accept the ones I have chosen. But be careful to use nouns, and whenever possible concrete nouns, because it is easiest to form a connection with them. But when you have made your choice you must stick to it thereafter.

While, in this case, it is unnecessary to list a secondary series, I will give you one because in a later chapter I am giving you a parlour game based on this secondary series. For this purpose I have not always chosen the simplest and most obvious words, but only those which may be used in a room where tables are laid out for a party. I have also added my associations for the reader if he is interested. The secondary series of words reads:

1. tea	—cup	(a cup of tea)
2. Noah	—boat	(the Ark of Noah was the first boat)
3. May	—pole	(Maypole)
4. ray	—bulb	(an electric bulb emits rays)
5. law	—ruler	(a good ruler enforces the law)
6. Shaw	—book	(Shaw wrote many books)
7. key	—pencil	(She carried her key and a pencil in her bag)
8. fee	—bill	(The fee is added to the bill)

9. bay	—water	(There is water in the bay)
10. tease	—trick	(To tease a person you play a trick on him)
11. tot	—doll	(The tiny tot has a doll)
12. tan	—leather	(Some leather is tan in colour)
13. team	—game	(The team played a game)
14. tar	—feather	(Tarred and feathered)
15. tale	—letter	(The letter told a tale)
16. touch	—material	(By touch you can tell the kind of material)
17. tack	—pin	(Tacks and pins are somewhat similar)
18. toffee	—chocolate	(Toffee and chocolate are confectionery)
19. tap	—beer	(You can draw beer from a tap)
20. niece	—picture	(A picture of my niece)
21. net	—veil	(A net veil)
22. noon	—watch	(My watch tells me it is noon)
23. name	—visiting card	(My name is on my visiting card)
24. Nero	—cigarette lighter	(Nero burned Rome. Fire reminds me of cigarette lighter)
25. nail	—file	(A nail-file)
26. niche	—vase	(The vase is in a niche)
27. neck	—tie	(necktie)
28. nave	—ring	(In the nave the bride received the ring)
29. nap	—napkin	(Nap and napkin are similar in sound)
30. mass	—candle	(Candles are burned at Mass)
31. mat	—rug	(They are alike)
32. man	—cigar	(The man smokes cigars)
33. mama	—jewellery	(Mama wears jewellery)
34. mare	—whip	(Mare and whip belong together)
35. mail	—stamp	(Mail and stamp belong together)
36. match	—box	(Matchbox)

37. mike	—radio	(Belong together)
38. muff	—glove	(In winter one wears gloves and a muff)
39. map	—calendar	(A map and a calendar hang on the wall)
40. race	—notebook	(At a horse race one needs a book to note the winner)
41. rat	—trap	(The rat was caught in a trap)
42. rain	—umbrella	(In the rain you need an umbrella)
43. ram	—tobacco	(Tobacco is rammed in a pipe)
44. rear	—book end	(Rear and end have a similar meaning)
45. rail	—metal	(Rails are made of metal)
46. rash	—food	(Rash sounds like rasher—a rasher of bacon is food)
47. rake	—tool	(A rake is a tool)
48. reef	—cord	(Reef—cable—cord)
49. rap	—cane	(A rap with a cane)
50. lace	—handker-chief	(The lace on a handkerchief)
51. lot	—money	(A lot of money)
52. lane	—stone	(The lane is paved with stone)
53. lime	—fruit	(The lime is a fruit)
54. lair	—flashlight	(The lair is in a cave; to see in the cave you need a flashlight)
55. lull	—pillow	(During a lull in activity you rest on a pillow)
56. lash	—ashtray	(Similar in sound)
57. lake	—bathing dress	(To swim in the lake you need a bathing dress)
58. leaf	—flower	(Leaf and flower belong together)
59. lap	—handbag	(A woman puts her handbag on her lap, for instance in the cinema)
60. chase	—silver	(Silver is sometimes chased)
61. chat	—lipstick	(Chat—lady—mouth—lipstick)
62. chain	—string	(Chain and string are similar)

63. chime —bell (The chime of the bell)
64. chair —furniture (A chair is a piece of furniture)
65. chill —ice (Chill and ice belong together)
66. judge —inkstand (On the judge's desk is an ink-stand)
67. cheque —pen (You write a cheque with a pen)
68. chaff —bread (chaff—wheat—flour—bread)
69. chap —cigarette (The young chap smokes cigarettes)
70. case —folder (A case and a folder both are used to hold valuable papers)

71. cat —fur (cat fur)
72. can —spoon (The fruit is taken from the can with a spoon)
73. cam —wheel (Belong together)
74. car —card (Similar in sound)
75. call —telephone (Telephone call)
76. cash —coin (Coins are cash)
77. cake —beverage (With cake you need a beverage)
78. cuff —button (Cuff-button)
79. cap —hat (Caps and hats are similar)
80. face —compact (A compact is used for the face)
81. fate —telegram (Telegrams often determine one's fate)

82. fan —thermom-eter (A fan is used when the thermom-eter is high)

83. fame —medal (A man of fame often wears medals)

84. fare —ticket (You get a ticket when you pay your fare)

85. fall —stairs (He fell downstairs)
86. fish —fork (Fish are eaten with a fork)
87. fake —photograph (Photograph was faked)
88. fife —musical in-strument (The fife is a musical instrument)
89. fop —mirror (The fop looks in the mirror)
90. base —wood (The base was made of wood)

91. bat	—sports	(The bat is used in several sports)
92. ban	—playing card	(In some localities there is a ban on playing cards)
93. beam	—pipe	(When he smokes his pipe he is beaming)
94. bar	—glass	(There are glasses on the bar)
95. ball	—rubber	(Most balls are made of rubber)
96. batch	—newspaper	(A batch of newspapers)
97. back	—apparel	(You buy apparel for your back)
98. beef	—knife	(To cut beef you need a knife)
99. babe	—toy	(The baby has a toy)

This secondary series can be remembered easily after one or two readings. The underlying principle for learning figures of four digits is as follows: The basic series of key words always comes first; therefore it is used for the first 2 digits of the number.

The secondary series always comes second; therefore it is used for the last 2 digits of the 4-digit number. If the telephone number of my friend Smith is 4295, it is not translated by rain and ball, but by *rain* and *rubber*, since for the first 2 digits (42) the basic key word is chosen and for the second 2 digits (95) the word from the secondary series. Since "rubbers" are worn in the rain, the picture is easy to remember.

If his number were 9542, the words would be *ball* and *umbrella*, for the number 42 is now in the second place and consequently the secondary series is used for it. A picture of my friend Smith with a ball in one hand and an umbrella in the other strikes me as so ridiculous that I remember it.

This method prevents you from getting mixed up. By using a secondary series we can recall numbers of 4 digits as readily as we have heretofore recalled numbers of 2 digits with the aid of the basic series of key words.

Now let us turn to the problem of remembering numbers with 3 digits. Of course, we could use the method we used for numbers with 4 digits. But we have another possibility, which simplifies the task. We can proceed as follows. We memorise these adjectives:

1. thick	6. short
2. new	7. coarse
3. mild	8. fine
4. round	9. pretty
5. long	

Each of these adjectives, as you see, begins with a consonant corresponding to the numerical code. Also each adjective can, in the majority of cases, be used with a noun.

Now, if we want to remember a 3-digit number, the use of the adjective is simple. 162 is *thick chain*; 274 is a *new car*; 438 is a *round muff*; 625 is a *short nail*; 911 is a *pretty tot*.

Should an adjective, in an exceptional case, not fit the noun with which it is to be associated, there is no reason why you should not choose another starting with the same consonant.

For instance, instead of using *long* for 5 you can use *light* or *loud*. As long as we are working solely with 3-digit numbers (not with 5 or 6 digits), it does not matter whether we use the basic key words or the secondary key words. The concept *new handkerchief* gives us the number 250 as readily as does *new lace*.

TELEPHONE NUMBERS, INCLUDING EXCHANGES

One of the most frequent applications of four (or more)-digit figures is telephone numbers. We need them constantly, and it is rather annoying and time-wasting to look them up every time we want to ring somebody.

It should be almost superfluous to repeat that we have the choice between a combination of basic and secondary lists and the finding of new words, as described in the preceding pages. Basic and secondary lists have the advantage of always being there in our minds, whereas new words have the advantage of being chosen to fit the person whose number we wish to remember.

The current system in this country is all-figure dialling. That is, each number consists of eleven digits usually combining three elements: area, exchange, and subscriber, e.g.,

0121–643–4297

0171–947–5762

0121–743–8471

Some subscribers, however, still think of numbers consisting of an exchange name followed by, say, three, four, or five digits, e.g,

Collingwood 4382

Winsdale 74510

Let us see how each of these types can be handled.

1. The all-digit number is harder to remember only if one relies on the usual method of memorising, i.e., repetition. If one relies upon a memory system, the number is easier to remember once the system has been mastered. And the reader who has reached this stage in the book should now have mastered it.

Let us apply the number code to remembering the three all-digit numbers quoted above. The first one, for a wine and spirits retailer, is:

0121–643–4297

It requires no great effort of imagination to turn this into:

Sweetened sherry may ruin bouquet

0   12 16 4   3   4 29 7

Here are some further examples:

A London Hotel may be 0171-947-5762

City'(s) quiet **park location** (thinking of Hyde Park)
0 1   7   19 47 5 7 6 2

A police station may be 0121-743-8471

sight night crime every **week**day
0   1 2   1 74 3   8 4   7 1

A travel agency may be 0121-740-0841

West Indies cruise is offered
01 21   74 0 0 8 4 1

2. The number code can also be applied to the combinations both of subscriber number with exchange name and of subscriber number with the dialling code for that exchange.

Since we know that it is difficult to find a single word for a four-digit number, we can always use two words. This is illustrated by our translation of Collingwood 4382. Collingwood can be replaced by any meaningful word which resembles it. I could use: **colic, colitis, collapse, collar(bone), colleen, college, collie, colliery, colour, column,** etc.

If I substitute harmony for 43 and fun for 82, the telephone number Collingwood 4382 may be translated into:

Colour + harmony = **fun**

Of course, with both types of telephone numbers, translating the number (or exchange name and number) into a meaningful group of words is only one half of our problem. The other half is to associate the number with the person or firm whose number it is. The group of words or sentence that we use must fit the name of the telephone subscriber. How do we tackle this part of the problem?

One other number of the second type above will serve as a simple example. Let us suppose that Winsdale 74510 is the phone number of an imaginary Winsdale General Hospital. We can associate name and number by means of the following sentence combining what you hope to get at a hospital, i.e., rest and cure, with an indication of the name of the hospital.

Win cure holidays

Here is an example showing how to work with an all-digit number. For instance, 0171–575–0110 is the number of a law college. We can associate college and number as follows:

easy to get legal status
0 1 7 15 7 5 011 0

Try your hand at some numbers you want to remember, and apply both methods to find for yourself which of them comes most natural to you.

As you can see, we have many possible ways of re-membering telephone numbers; and just because our system is not rigid but very flexible, we can adjust it to any type of number we wish to remember. Since you can take your choice among all these possibilities, it will be easy for you to remember every number you need in business or private life. Make this your firm resolve: "I will never look up a number twice!"

CHAPTER XIX

HOW TO REMEMBER PLAYING CARDS

IF we wish to apply our system to playing cards without extra effort, we can associate the cards with our basic list of words. Before you read my suggestions on how to go about it, try to find a solution yourself. Since this idea may seem a little odd to you, here is the reason why you should.

Whatever your profession or occupation may be, you will face many problems which cannot be discussed and explained in this book. This is necessarily so because the book was written for the general public and not for specific individuals.

Therefore it will be most useful for you if you yourself check your ability, which should be rather well developed by now, in applying this system to something new, something which has not yet been discussed. What you find out for yourself in one or two hours is much more useful than reading a ready-made solution in a few minutes, as you can do in the following paragraphs.

Here is the solution: In a pack of playing cards there are four different suits, which we number in alphabetical order:

Clubs	1
Diamonds	2
Hearts	3
Spades	4

To each number we append the number of the card, that is, its real value. For instance:

Club 4   is 1 and 4, or 14
(or the 4 of clubs)
Diamond 7   is 2 and 7, or 27
(or the 7 of diamonds)
Heart 9   is 3 and 9, or 39
(or the 9 of hearts)
Spades 2   is 4 and 2, or 42
(or the 2 of spades)

The ace has one pip on its face and may therefore be valued as 1, while the easiest valuation of 10 is zero (0). Consequently:

Diamond ace   is 2 and 1, or 21
(or the ace of diamonds)
Hearts 10   is 3 and 0, or 30
(or the 10 of hearts)

Using this method, we arrive at numbers of two digits, for which we can substitute the key words of our basic list. If we do this with the cards listed above, we have:

The 4 of clubs is 14, or *tar*.
The 7 of diamonds is 27, or *neck*.
The 9 of hearts is 39, or *map*.
The 2 of spades is 42, or *rain*.
The ace of diamonds is 21, or *net*.
The 10 of hearts is 30, or *mass*.

Only the face cards remain. When we bring them into our system, we find that we have used only the first 49 words in our basic list. All the words between 50 and 100 are still free and at our disposal. Let us try this plan: For a face card, add 5 to the suit number. That will give us the following suit values for face cards:

Clubs	6
Diamonds	7
Hearts	8
Spades	9

The face cards themselves may be valued as follows:

Jack	2
Queen	3
King	4

If we follow the system we used for number cards, we arrive at these numbers:

Club Jack	is 6 and 2, or 62
(or the Jack of clubs)	
Diamond Queen	is 7 and 3, or 73
(or the Queen of diamonds)	
Spade King	is 9 and 4, or 94
(or the King of spades)	

This is the easiest way to connect playing cards with the basic list of words, and it should not be difficult for you to repeat, in order, the names of a full pack of cards which you looked through only once or which someone called out to you. To give an example, let us suppose that the first ten cards in a well-shuffled pack are the following:

   (1) 8 of clubs
   (2) 2 of spades
   (3) 5 of clubs
   (4) 2 of diamonds
   (5) 3 of diamonds
   (6) Queen of hearts
   (7) 5 of spades
   (8) 7 of hearts
   (9) King of diamonds
(10) 2 of hearts

It goes without saying that we have to handle the numbers which are substitutes for playing cards in the same way as we would handle other numbers; that is, we form the following connections:

(1) 8 of clubs, or 18, or **toffee** has to be connected with
                  the first word of the basic

list, which is **tea**. "I see **toffee** on the **tea**-table."

(2) 2 of spades, or 42, or **rain** has to be connected with the second word of the basic list, which is **Noah.** "**Noah** survived the Deluge, or **rain**."

(3) 5 of clubs, or 15, or **tale** has to be connected with the third word of the basic list, which is **May.** "**Many** a love **tale** starts in **May**."

Now, assuming that you understand the system, I shall give the connections only:

(4) "The **rays** of the sun are most intense at **noon**." (22, or the 2 of diamonds)

(5) "There is a **law** for changing one's **name**." (23, or the 3 of diamonds)

(6) "**Shaw** won **fame** as a writer." (83, or the Queen of hearts)

(7) "The **key** is hidden behind the stair **rail**." (45, or the 5 of spades)

(8) "The lecturer received a large **fee** for speaking into the **mike**." (37, or the 7 of hearts)

(9) "You can drive around the **bay** in a **car**." (74, or the King of diamonds)

(10) "Do not **tease** this **man**." (32, or the 2 of hearts)

Once you have impressed these connections upon your mind, you will find it easy to recall the playing cards by thinking through the list of words. In order to repeat the cards, proceed as follows:

1. The first word of the basic list is **tea**. With **tea** we

connected **toffee**. Toffee is 18, and 18 is the 8 of clubs.

2. The second word of the basic list is **Noah**. With **Noah** we connected **rain**. Rain is 42, and 42 is the 2 of spades.

3. The third word of the basic list is **May**. With **May** we connected **tale.** Tale is 15, and 15 is the 5 of clubs. And so on.

If you master the list of words, you will face no difficulties. There is only one way to prove it: Try it!

REMEMBERING PLAYING CARDS IN CONNECTION WITH PERSONS

This experiment combines the training of your memory for playing cards with developing a sound memory for names. It is much more interesting than the foregoing, but it is also more difficult. Therefore, do not attempt it until you can remember the cards in sequence. The experiment goes this way: Suppose that you are at a party with ten other persons. Their names, and I have chosen the real names of some of my students, are:

Mr. Black
Mr. Lynch
Miss Warter
Mr. Caine
Mr. Gold
Miss Adams
Mr. Singer
Mr. Goodstein
Mr. Tunis
Mrs. Fields

Each of them takes one card at random and tells you which card he holds. Let us assume that the cards are distributed as follows:

Mr. Black	5 of hearts
Mr. Lynch	4 of diamonds
Miss Warter	ace of diamonds
Mr. Caine	2 of hearts
Mr. Gold	Jack of clubs
Miss Adams	3 of diamonds
Mr. Singer	10 of hearts
Mr. Goodstein	5 of clubs
Mr. Tunis	King of diamonds
Mrs. Fields	5 of spades

The ability to remember which card each person holds is based on the same principle as the ability to remember the cards in sequence.

Again we translate the card into a number, and the number into the corresponding word of the basic list. But instead of connecting this word with our list of words, we connect it with the name of the person who is holding the card.

So, we may form associations like this:

1. Mr. Black has the 5 of hearts. The 5 of hearts is 35, or **mail**. As a connection we may use the word **blackmail**.

2. Mr. Lynch has the 4 of diamonds. The 4 of diamonds is 24, or **Nero.** We think of Nero as a tyrant who murdered, or **lynched**, many persons.

3. Miss Warter has the ace of diamonds. The name "Warter" has no meaning in itself. Therefore we substitute **water**, which is quite similar in sound. She is holding the ace of diamonds, which is 21, or **net**. If we imagine a fisherman's net in the **water**, we have an easy connection.

Assuming that you understand this procedure fully, I am condensing the following associations:

4. Mr. Caine has the 2 of hearts. For "Caine"

substitute **cane**. The 2 of hearts: man. "A **man** carries a **cane**."

5. Mr. Gold has the Jack of clubs; that is, a chain: "a **gold chain**."

6. Miss Adams has the 3 of diamonds; that is, name: "**Adam** was the **name** of the first man."

7. Mr. Singer has the 10 of hearts: mass. "He **sings** at **mass**."

8. Mr. Goodstein has the 5 of clubs: tale. "A **good tale**."

9. Mr. Tunis has the King of diamonds: car. Visualise a **car** at army headquarters in **Tunis**.

10. Mrs. Fields has the 5 of spades: rail. Visualise **rails** of a railway stretching through **fields**.

Obviously, it is easier to make this experiment with persons whom you know than with strangers. The reason is that we have no difficulty in forming associations with persons familiar to us because there are many things we can connect with them. For instance, besides the name we can associate occupation or profession, character traits, hobbies, some expression of personal opinion, or countless other items.

If, however, we are making this experiment with strangers, we have nothing to go on but the name and appearance of the person in question. Therefore our task is more difficult. On the other hand, it affords better training. So try it first with acquaintances and then with strangers, and gradually increase the number of persons from ten to fifty-two—the number of playing cards in a pack.

That this experiment has a practical value far beyond its apparently frivolous character will be shown in the next chapter.

CHAPTER XX

CONNECTING PERSONS WITH FACTS OR QUESTIONS

IN Chapter XII, in reference to another subject, I stressed the importance of remembering certain facts, statements, or questions in connection with a group of persons.

As examples of this contingency in everyday life, let me cite the instance of a speaker who finds it necessary to answer in his finishing remarks, after a debate, statements or questions raised during the discussion. Let me also point to the advantageous position a chairman finds himself in if he can remember the suggestions or desires of the persons attending the convention or meeting—and not only the suggestions themselves, but also the persons who made them.

If we compare such a feat of memory with the playing-card experiment described in the preceding chapter, we can claim with calm assurance that it is not harder but, rather, easier than the latter.

It is easier because no linking thought is necessary, as there is between the playing card and the word in the basic list; and the associations are simpler anyway, for the various questions or remarks are all in the same general field and therefore simpler to connect. Otherwise the method employed is the same.

To furnish a practical example, let us make these assumptions: the persons mentioned in the preceding chapter are again gathered together; a lecture entitled

"The Art of Public Address" is being delivered to them; and some of those present ask questions and make remarks which they would like to have treated in a comprehensive at the end of the lecture. We think it especially important to know, with each reply, the name of the person who asked the question originally.

In order to accomplish this feat, proceed as follows:

1. Mr. Black asks: "Is it necessary for me to make an outline before I start working out the address itself?" In order to remember the person who asked the question and the question itself, visualising an **outline** written in **black** ink might suffice.

2. Miss Warter asks: "Should I rely on a manuscript when I deliver a speech?" Association: see a **manuscript** floating on **water** (water being a substitute for Warter).

3. Mr. Gold asks how to go about collecting material for a speech. Association: **Gold** is the most precious **material** in the world.

4. Miss Adams asks how to make clear the aim and purpose of a speech. Association: **Adam**, the first man— **aim and purpose** of mankind.

5. Mr. Singer asks how to limit a speech to the time allotted to it. Association: Every **song** (song as a substitute for singer) requires a certain length of **time**.

6. Mr. Tunis asks how to keep an audience from growing restive. Association: **Tunis**—battle—tension— **restive**.

Following this procedure, any number of questions may be asked by any number of people. When the

question period has come to an end and we are to begin
with the answers, it is absolutely necessary to take the
name of the questioner as the point of departure in
order to get on the right path of association, in our
accustomed manner, between the person and the question he or she asked.

When we look at Mr. Black, we immediately reconstruct the association Black—black ink—outline. When
we look at Miss Warter, water will come to mind, then a
manuscript floating on water.

Here, as in all preceding chapters, theory will not do
the trick. It needs training and I can only advise everyone to seize every available opportunity in business and
private life to put the theory into practice.

Up to this point we have confined ourselves to
remembering questions and associating these questions
with the persons who asked them. How to reply to the
questions remains to be discussed. Two possibilities
present themselves.

The simpler one is to answer the questions singly
without regard for any relationship among them and,
in so doing, reply to the questioners in the order in
which they are seated.

The more difficult one is to assemble the questions in
our minds, before answering, in such a way that the
answers themselves constitute a logically arranged
speech or story. This, of course, is the goal of every
lecturer, chairman, or president of a meeting.

Miss Irene Baker and Mr. Frank Murray, two of my
students, were able to answer about thirty questions in
coherent and excellent speeches, even before their course
was completed. And many others among my students
are capable of doing the same.

As an example of how the questions listed above
can be answered in an orderly, logical way, I refer

you to Chapter XXV of this book, which contains the solution.

Finally, the following is to be noted: In rare individual cases it may be necessary to remember the remarks or questions in the exact order in which they were uttered. I need hardly call attention to the fact that in these cases the basic list of words must be put to use. In the example given above, the following connections should be set up:

(1) tea   —outline
(2) Noah—manuscript
(3) May   —material
(4) ray   —aim and purpose
(5) law   —time
(6) Shaw—restive

This method is obviously the more difficult. Yet the need for applying it in everyday life is rather rare.

On the other hand, the method for associating remarks or questions with a speaker or questioner in everyday life is easier than reading about it in this chapter would indicate. The reason is as follows: Since my readers do not themselves know the persons I chose as questioners, I was forced to take their names alone as points of departure.

In reality, however, a speaker or chairman of the evening knows many of the assembled group personally, so that the connection need not necessarily be made with the name of the questioner but may be made with his business, traits of character, hobbies, or the like—a procedure which, as I mentioned at the end of the previous chapter, makes the association much easier. But even in dealing with strangers, a connection with the appearance of the questioner, or with the place from which he is asking the question, is considerably easier than a connection with his name.

If you put this experiment into practice and thereby astound an audience, please let me know about your triumphs.

CHAPTER XXI

ECONOMISING TIME IN LEARNING
THE INTERNATIONAL MORSE CODE

"COULDN'T these dots and dashes be arranged in a simple, methodical way instead of being so hit-and-miss?"

This is the constant complaint of the thousands of would-be telegraphers and radio operators who are studying the International Morse Code. It is the complaint, too, of persons who plan to use the code for signalling, sending messages by heliograph, and operating other communication facilities.

In spite of a deep interest in the subject, many prospective students have become discouraged after one or two futile attempts to memorise the dots and dashes which the International Morse Code uses to represent the various letters in the alphabet.

Before a person can learn how to send and receive messages by telegraph, he must memorise the twenty-six letters in the alphabet in code. The purpose of this chapter is to present a simple yet interesting way to do it.

This is what the alphabet looks like in code:

A	.—	G	——.
B	—...	H	....
C	—.—.	I	..
D	—..	J	.———
E	.	K	—.—
F	..—.	L	.—..

M	——	T	—
N	—·	U	··—
O	———	V	···—
P	·——·	W	·——
Q	——·—	X	—··—
R	·—·	Y	—·——
S	···	Z	——··

You need only to glance at the assortment of dots and dashes to appreciate the beginner's dismay. There is no uniformity in sequence. There is no pattern. Taken all in all, the code presents a confusing picture, and it is not easy to memorise.

If a good system or memory aid were developed to facilitate memorising the alphabet in code, the beginner would feel encouraged to go on with his task.

A number of methods or aids have been suggested, but none has been found satisfactory in practice, either because they required too great a knowledge of mnemonics or because they included too many exceptions to the rules laid down.

Here is my suggestion for a method by which you can commit the code to memory in fifteen or twenty minutes. Let us proceed step by step:

STEP 1. For each letter of the alphabet we substitute a specific word. Each word begins with the letter of the alphabet it represents. Later on we shall see how easily these words can be transposed into the code. The following words, which we call "cue words" or "cue word combinations," represent the letters:

A ir	F iery
B ruise	G lobe
C hina	H is essay
D ray	I ssue
E sso	J ust now

K odak	S usie
L ydia	T ot
M onk	U sual
N ote	V isual
O n top	W ith
P arty	X-rays
Q-Club	Y okels
R eno	Z ombie

The average student should be able to memorise these words in alphabetical order, as presented, in ten minutes. But he can make his exercise in memory still easier by incorporating the words into this little five-sentence story which uses them consecutively:

A shell burst in the *Air*, causing a *Bruise* to a soldier in *China*, who was riding in a *Dray*.

The soldier, Private *Esso*, wrote about the *Fiery Globe*. *His essay* is at *Issue Just now*.

With his *Kodak* he took pictures of *Lydia* and a *Monk* writing a *Note On top* of a hill.

Then he went to a *Party* at the *Q-Club* in *Reno*, taking *Susie* and her *Tot* along as *Usual*.

At the club, *Visual with X-rays* were *Yokels* acting like a *Zombie*.

Once this odd story is learned, it is easy to remember. So are the cue words, because they appear in alphabetical order and each representative, or cue word, acts as an association for the succeeding cue word. Thus each word brings the next word to mind.

STEP 2. Having learned the cue words, apply the following rules: The first letter of each word is used merely to indicate the letter of the alphabet being coded. For the succeeding letters, substitute a dot (.) for each vowel (a e i o u y); and substitute a dash (—) for each consonant. For example:

A ir   C hina

  • ━   ━ • ━ •

However, the letters *s* and *o* are substituted for a dot
or dash *only when they appear at the end of a cue word or
cue word combination*. In all other positions they are
disregarded. *s* and *o* are easily remembered by thinking
of sos. For example:

H is essay   R eno

 • • ••   • ━ •

The *s* in *His* does not count because it is not at the end
of the cue word combination. The *o* in *Reno* counts
because it is at the end of the cue word.

The entire alphabet is thus transposed as follows:

ir	ydia
A •━	L •━••
ruise	onk
B ━•••	M ━━
hina	ote
C ━•━•	N ━•
ray	n top
D ━••	O ━━━
sso	arty
E •	P •━━•
iery	Club
F ••━•	Q ━━•━
lobe	eno
G ━━•	R •━•
is essay	usie
H ••••	S • ••
ssue	ot
I ••	T ━
ust now	sual
J •━━━	U ••━
odak	isual
K ━•━	V •••━

ith	okels
W .——	Y —.——
rays	ombie
X —..—	Z ——..

If you have followed the instructions carefully, you should now know the symbol in the Morse Code for each letter in the alphabet.

For learning numbers in the Morse Code, no memory aid is necessary. They are coded in a clear pattern, as follows:

(1)	.————	(6)	—....
(2)	..———	(7)	——...
(3)	...——	(8)	———..
(4)	....—	(9)	————.
(5)	.....	(0)	—————

You will note that the numbers from 1 to 5 start with from 1 to 5 dots, and the numbers from 6 to 0 start with from 1 to 5 dashes. All are supplemented by the opposite symbol to a total of five. This uniform progression is easy to learn without any aid to memory.

The use of the International Morse Code is not confined to telegraphy. It extends to simpler forms of communication, such as signalling with flags, heliographs, and flash and blinker lights. Our little story of five sentences will give the memory aid needed for all of these.

CHAPTER XXII

MNEMOTECHNICAL GAMES

You can now repeat without error a series of 100 or 200 words and figures after having heard them once, and you can also effortlessly call any chosen word or number out of its proper order.

In addition, you have read short summaries of several cases showing practical application in all sorts of fields of study and in everyday life.

Before going on with the serious study of mnemotechny, I would like to demonstrate to you some of its amusing possibilities. By way of review, therefore, of what you have already learned, I am going to introduce you to some entertaining parlour games which you will find it interesting to try out on your friends.

But stimulating and enjoyable as these games are, I should not introduce them at this point if I had no serious reason for doing so. As a matter of fact, these games develop your powers of concentration. Every exercise in mnemotechny is in the final analysis an exercise in concentration, no matter for what reason it is undertaken.

One of the most interesting games that can be played with the aid of mnemotechny, and one that baffles the uninitiated spectator, is so-called "mind reading." *It naturally has nothing to do with actual telepathy*. It is merely the application of what we have already learned.

This game presupposes that you instruct one other person in the system outlined in this book. You both know key words and secondary series. So you both know that 91 is sports.

In other words, if you were to call out number 91 to your partner, he would answer **sports**. But such a stunt would be too obvious to all those present and we shall therefore try to change it so that it will lose its transparency. This is not difficult. It can be done as follows:

Instead of calling out "91" you can call "9 . . . 1."
Instead of "9 . . . 1" you can say "**p,t.**"

And instead of saying "**p,t,**" you can form a sentence in which the first two words begin with the consonants *p* and *t*.

For instance, "**P**lease **t**ell me what I have in my hand." Your partner knows he must pay attention only to the initial consonant in each of the first two words and that the rest of the sentence is a matter of no consequence to him. So he pays attention to "**P**lease **t**ell" only and takes the consonants *p* and *t*. He knows that these mean 9 . . . 1 and therefore 91, and he knows, in addition, that the number 91 in the secondary series is *sports*. With this information he can answer your apparently artless question with the correct name of the object you hold in your hand.

In this case your task is somewhat more difficult than your partner's, for you must word your question, seemingly casually, in such a way that the first two words have the right initial consonants. Your partner's task is simpler. He need know only the secondary series in order to give the correct answer immediately. And, you see, the secondary series contains practically all the words necessary for a social gathering.

Since those present invariably hold out a great number of objects when you ask for them, you always have the opportunity to choose acceptable things and disregard those not listed in our secondary series.

In order to avert any misunderstanding in formulating questions, here are a few additional examples: "Can you tell what I have in my hand?" would mean 71. The second word, *you*, consists of vowels and is therefore not counted. For the same reason, "Can you please tell me . . ." means 79.

"May I ask you . . ." is 30.

"Let me know . . ." is 53, etc.

With a little practice you will not find it difficult to construct questions using numbers from 1 to 100.

Furthermore, this very pleasant little game is not confined to objects in our series, but can be extended in the same way to other things, such as coins and cards.

In the case of coins, the game revolves around their value as well as their date of coinage. For their date you naturally think of our old mnemotechnical principle of simplification and confine yourself to the last two ciphers. Mistakes will not occur, for if the last two ciphers are greater than the last two digits of the current year, the coins have been minted in the previous century, that is, in the 1800's. If they are below, their date begins with 1900. As an example:

"**Please c**an you tell me the date of this coin!" means 1897. The words "Please can" give the initiated the figures 9 and 7, or 97. The 18 he can of course supply himself and reach 1897.

The question "**N**ow **g**ive me the date on this coin," means "*n,g,*" therefore 27. The completion of the date with 19 is a matter of common sense, since coins minted in 1827 are no longer in circulation. So the person asked can safely supply the answer 1927.

In a similar way, the initiated can play this mnemotechnical question-and-answer game with playing cards. To play this game, use the rules given in Chapter XIX for playing cards generally. Remember that we used the suits in alphabetical order with the following number values:

Clubs	1
Diamonds	2
Hearts	3
Spades	4

The questions are then put in the same fashion as in the examples for objects and coins. The initial consonant of the *first* word tells the suit; the initial consonant of the *second* word tells the value of the card. Do not forget that we valued the 10 as 0, and the ace as 1. Remember, also, that we numbered the face cards as follows:

Jack	2
Queen	3
King	4

In order to distinguish the face cards from the other cards in the pack, we added 5 to the suit-number. If you have forgotten these details, read Chapter XIX again.

If you have the values of the suit-numbers and the face cards well in mind, you will quickly figure out the following:

Question: "Now let me know what this card is!" Answer: "The 5 of diamonds." The first word starts with **n**, giving you the second suit—diamonds. The second word starts with **l**, giving you the value of the card—5. Therefore the answer is "The 5 of diamonds."

Question: "Read now this card!" *Read* starts with **r**; therefore it is the fourth suit, or spades. *Now* starts with **n**; therefore it is the number 2. Answer: "The 2 of spades."

Question: "Give me the name of this card!" *Give* starts with **g**; and **g** is 7, or a diamond and face card; *me* starts with **m**, which is 3, or the Queen. Since I know that the card is a face card, the answer must be "The Queen of diamonds."

There is another possibility in connection with the face cards. Instead of adding 5 to the suit, we can agree upon a certain word which will always indicate that we are dealing with a face card.

For instance, we might use the word *attention*. In that case, the addition of 5 is unnecessary, and the suit-number can always remain the same. The **t** in *attention*, of course, does not count. The question, "Tell me what card I have in my hand!" calls for the answer, "The 3 of clubs." (**t** means clubs; **m** means 3.) "Attention, tell me what card I have in my hand!" calls for "The Queen of clubs," because **t** means clubs, and **m** means Queen, since the word *attention* indicates a face card.

But I should like to call attention to the fact that this "little game" has a dangerous side to it, for similar methods are used by experienced card-sharpers to inform partners which cards to lead.

Remember that the information need not be given in the form of a question and that it need not be related to the cards themselves. For instance, if a player makes the apparently casual remark: "My telephone has been out of order," his partner understands he is to lead the ace of hearts. The *M* in "My" tells him the suit, hearts, and the initial consonant *t* in "telephone," the ace.

So be on your guard against card-sharpers, for, like everything else that is good, mnemotechny can be used for evil purposes.

CHAPTER XXIII

REMEMBERING DATES AND RECKONING THE DAY OF THE WEEK

OCCASIONALLY in everyday life it is necessary to remember not only a certain year but even a specific date. In such instances, however, we can assume that the century is always so well known that it need not be recalled. If a certain day is so important that you want to keep the exact date in mind, you can hardly be in doubt about the century to which it belongs.

Our task, therefore, is to combine in some way the month, the day of the month, and the last two figures of the year. Combining two 2-figure numbers presents no difficulty, for we have a basic series and a secondary series of words at our command. But what shall we do about the third number?

The nine adjectives, representing the figures from 1 to 9, which we have already learned, can be used for the months from January to September, inclusive, so that April, the fourth month, will be replaced by the adjective *round*. Then all we have to do is to add three more adjectives for the figures 10, 11, and 12, that is, the months October, November and December. These adjectives must produce the figures 10, 11 and 12 when we translate their consonants into numbers. For instance:

10. various adjectives that begin with **dis**: discoloured, discovered, etc.
11. *tight*
12. *thin*

If we *always* substitute the *adjective for the month*, the word from the basic series of key words for the day of the month, and the word from the secondary series for the year, no confusion will ever arise.

September 11, 1872, is translated as follows:

September, the 9th month, is *pretty*.
11 in the basic series of key words is *tot*.
72 in the secondary series of words is *spoon*.
September 11, 1872, therefore is: *A pretty tot with a spoon*.

Another example: December 25, 1890:

December, the 12th month, is *thin*.
25 in the basic series of key words is *nail*.
90 in the secondary series is *wood*.
December 25, 1890, is therefore: *A thin nail in wood*.

There is a variant for this method which you may prefer. We are accustomed to associate some quite definite thing with each month, that is, we have a symbol in mind for each month, usually the same for the majority of people.

For instance, everybody thinks of Christmas in connection with December and consequently of the symbol *Christmas tree*. By using these symbols we can dispense with the adjective and substitute the particular symbol for the month. The example given above would then read: December 25, 1890: *Christmas tree—nail—wood*. This combination is easy to remember since a Christmas tree is often nailed to a wood stand.

I shall return later to the symbols for the various months, but at this point I want to urge you to choose your own symbols. For instance, if a person was born in December, he will find himself a better symbol than the tree. The choice in this instance resolves itself into a practical matter determined by individual factors. I naturally had to rely on my general knowledge of the average man in choosing my symbols.

In any case, remember that in this system *the serial order of the concepts is of no importance:*

The adjective or the symbol is *always* the month.

The basic series of key words is *always* the day of the month.

The secondary series of words is *always* the year.

In connection with this method for remembering dates, I want to give you also a simple way of reckoning dates, that is, a method by which it is possible to determine the day of the week for any date you choose, even though it be several centuries in the past.

What I have repeated so often in this book is again true: without mnemotechny this task is very difficult; with mnemotechnical aid it is comparatively easy.

First we give each month a special number, which has nothing to do with the calendar. For remembering them I shall later give you mnemotechnical aid. These numbers are:

January	4	July	2
February	0	August	5
March	6	September	1
April	2	October	3
May	4	November	6
June	0	December	1

Then we number the days consecutively, beginning with Sunday:

Sunday	1
Monday	2
Tuesday	3
Wednesday	4
Thursday	5
Friday	6
Saturday	7

If we continued numbering, with 8 we would come again to Sunday; 9, Monday; 10, Tuesday, etc. At 15 we should again have Sunday and once more at 22. From this we conclude we may discard the number 7 and every multiple of 7, without affecting our computations.

For instance, 37 is 2, because the number 37 equals 5 times 7 plus 2. In other words, if at 1 we start with Sunday and number the days consecutively, at 37 we reach Monday. We can simplify the matter by disregarding five times seven (the multiple of 7) and merely use the remainder 2, which is Monday.

We use the same method both for the day of the month and the year. For the months, we use the numerical code given above.

But so far we have completely disregarded the century. For instance, if we had April 10, 1822, our computation would run as follows:

April (according to the code given above)	equals	2
10 equals seven plus three (disregarding the 7 for reasons given above)	„	3
The year 1822 (leaving the century out of our reckoning) equals 22; 3 × 7 plus 1	„	1
	Total	6

That gives us the sixth day, or Friday.

But this result is not correct, because up to now we have not considered the leap years. To reckon correctly, we divide the last 2 figures of the year (the century is again disregarded) by 4 and add to it the result attained so far. Completely disregard any remainder. So we say: 22 divided by 4 equals 5 (the remainder 2 does not count) and add this 5 to the total of 6. We get 11, and since we can always drop 7, the result is 4. *This is a Wednesday*. We have reckoned quite correctly. *April 10, 1822, was a Wednesday.*

Suppose the date to be March 13, 1891. Then—

March, according to our code for the months	equals	6
13 equals 7 plus 6, therefore	,,	6
91 equals 13 × 7 (no remainder)	,,	0
91 divided by 4 equals 22 (disregard the remainder)		
22 equals 3 × 7 plus 1, therefore	,,	1
	Total	13

13 equals 7 plus 6; 6 is Friday
Therefore *March 13, 1891, was a Friday*

And now we come to a general exception: *January and February* must *always* be reckoned with the *preceding year*. For instance, February 10, 1939, must be reckoned as though it were February 10, 1938. Example:

William Pitt the Younger died Jan. 23, 1806.

January	equals	4
23 equals 3 × 7, remainder 2	,,	2
1806, reckoned as 1805, because the date falls in January; 05 equals 0 × 7, remainder 5	,,	5
05 divided by 4 equals 1. And 1 equals 0 × 7 plus 1, therefore	,,	1
	Total	12

12 equals 1 × 7, remainder 5; 5 *equals Thursday.*

William Pitt the Younger died on a *Thursday*.

But the century cannot always be disregarded, as in the case of the nineteenth century. In the present century, the twentieth, we must add the number 5, after we have carried the computations to this point; and there are four of these arbitrary numbers to remember.

The following general rule holds true:

If the first 2 figures of the century can be divided by 4 (for instance, 16—), we add 4. For the following century

(17—) we add 2. For the following century (18—) we add 0. (It was for this reason we could heretofore disregard the century.) For the following century (19—) we add 5.

These four numbers, 4-2-0-5, we remember with mnemotechnical aid, by using the numerical code *r-n-s-l* and note for remembrance, "The centuries **run** easily."

Here are a few more examples of how to reckon the day of the week:

John Evelyn, the diarist, died February 27, 1706.

February	equals	0
27 equals 3 × 7, remainder 6	,,	6
1700 as the century	,,	2
Instead of 1706, we reckon with 05, since we are dealing with February. 05 equals 0 × 7, remainder 5	,,	5
05 divided by 4 equals 1. And 1 equals 0 × 7 plus 1, therefore	,,	1
	Total	14

14 equals 1 × 7, remainder 7; 7 *equals Saturday.*

John Evelyn died on a *Saturday.*

The 25th anniversary of Queen Elizabeth II's coronation was on June 2, 1978.

June	equals	0
2	,,	2
1900 as century	,,	5
78 equals 11 × 7, remainder	,,	1
78 divided by 4	,,	19
	Total	27

27 (minus 3 × 7) equals 6

June 2, 1978, fell on *Friday.*

Now, only the code for the months remains to be learned, for which I promised you mnemotechnical aid. You can use these symbols for remembering dates, too, as I mentioned at the beginning of this chapter. The first consonant of the code word, which agrees in every case with the initial consonant of the symbol for the month, gives you the numerical code for reckoning dates.

January	New Year's Day	Year or Era	4
February	St. Valentine's Day	Sweetheart	0
March	St. Patrick's Day	Shamrock	6
April	April Fool's Day	Naïve	2
May	V.E. Day	Europe	4
June	June 21, longest day	Summer begins	0
July	St. Swithin's Day	No rain	2
August	Bank Holiday	Holiday	5
September	Autumn commences	Autumn	1
October	Trafalgar Day	Maritime	3
November	Bonfire Night	Jolly	6
December	Christmas	Tree	1

And now let us try to simplify this whole system for practical everyday use. The value in *workaday life* consists merely in being able to know immediately *every day in the current year, the year past, the one to come.*

If this is the goal we set for ourselves, we can simplify our computations to a great degree by noting the results for these three years.

Take 1985 for instance. As we saw from the last example,

1900 (the century)	equals	5
85 equals 12 × 7, remainder	,,	1
85 divided by 4 equals 21: 21	,,	0
	Total	6

1985 is 6.

If we keep 6 in mind, working out any given date in the year 1985 is a matter of seconds and can be done mentally.

July 27, 1985, for instance, is

July	equals	2
27	,,	6
1985	,,	6
		—
	Total	14

14 is 1×7, remainder 7; therefore Saturday.

In the same way we can arrive at the results for the following years:

$$1986 : 0$$
$$1987 : 1$$
$$1988 : 3$$

Christmas Day, 1986, is on Thursday:

December	equals	1
25	,,	4
1986	,,	0
		—
	Total	5 which is Thursday.

PART TWO

THE ART OF PUBLIC ADDRESS

CHAPTER XXIV

THE APPLICATION OF MNEMOTECHNY TO PUBLIC SPEAKING

AFTER these little mnemotechnical games we turn again to the sober realities of life. There are few things more important for the practical man of affairs than the ability to make a speech to a large gathering of his fellows.

You know from your own experience that people with the so-called gift of speech usually are leaders in their clubs and lodges and, most important of all, in business gatherings.

There are many professions, indeed, based largely or entirely on speech-making abilities, such as the law or politics. With the growth in importance of the radio and TV in influencing public opinion, the ability to make effective public speeches has become more and more desirable.

Throughout our history the words of great speeches go echoing, words which swayed and influenced those who heard them, such as Sir Winston Churchill's challenging speeches in World War II.

The first demand made on a speaker is that he be able to make his address extemporaneously, without manuscript. It is not too much to say that it is *impossible* to make a good speech if one has his eyes glued on a manuscript. The verbatim reading of a typed manuscript can never equal an extemporaneous address.

The speech read from a script lacks the living quality

of the extemporaneous address. In the latter the audience follows the speaker in his thought-processes and searches with him for the exact, apt word. The natural sentence structure is entirely different in speaking from that in writing, and the written speech has longer sentences than the address.

A listener can understand the trend of thought more easily when he has helped, as it were, in its formation. It is more difficult for him when he merely listens to sentences styled, beforehand, away from an actual audience.

In fact, the influence of the audience on the speaker should not be underrated. Even without interruptions or spontaneous applause or signs of disapproval, the speaker can read from the countenances of the audience how far they understand his address and agree or disagree with him. And he will be able to shape the rest of his speech according to their reaction. But if he wishes to get a reaction from his audience, two basic principles must be established:

First, he must not be hampered by a set speech prepared beforehand, for then there is no chance for him to make changes and he cannot introduce a new thought because he cannot stray from his manuscript.

Secondly, a speaker must look at his audience occasionally, to get the play of expression on their countenances. His eyes must be free to look at his public, not riveted on his manuscript. The speaker should realise that his eyes are as important as his voice, and that expressive eyes augment the impression made by his voice, or even replace it.

The listener, who has to keep his eyes fastened on the mouth of the speaker, can also demand that the latter, in turn, occasionally look at his public, instead of merely reading from a manuscript.

If the speaker is able to answer heckling without losing the thread of his discourse, he shows presence of mind and ready wit. For example, this little story is told about a certain eloquent politician:

He was constantly interrupted by a man in the crowd who kept shouting, "Liar!" After about the twentieth repetition, the speaker paused and fixed his eye on the heckler. "If the gentleman who persists in interrupting," he said, "will be good enough to tell us his name instead of merely shouting out his profession, I am sure we shall all be pleased to make his acquaintance."

Such ready wit in answering, combined with the immediate resumption of a speech, is possible only for extemporaneous speakers who are not fettered by a manuscript. But the good speaker should catch and turn to his own advantage not only heckling but even the inarticulate responses of his audience.

The speaker who pays attention to the expressions on his listeners' faces very soon notices whether he is being completely understood or whether he need elaborate a part of his speech. From their countenances he can also see whether he is boring them by going into too many details, or whether, on the contrary, he has condensed a certain passage too much and should amplify it. But all this is possible *only if he keeps his eyes on his public*.

So the man who merely reads an address in public has really no right to be called a "speaker."

The very same thing holds true for the man who has learned his address *verbatim*. There is nothing so devastating for the speaker as to lose his place. And the ever-present fear of getting stuck is bound to affect his speech. With a partially learned address, the speaker suffers the additional fear of perhaps not being able to find his place when his memory fails him.

There are many other reasons why the extemporaneous speech is to be preferred to the written manuscript. But let this aspect of the matter suffice:

In the extemporaneous address, the speaker always seems to be drawing from a great reservoir of learning. While he is framing his sentences freely as he goes along, he unconsciously gives the impression of having an inexhaustible store of knowledge, of which he has tapped but a small portion of what he really has at his disposal.

Exactly the opposite impression is created by the manuscript reader. When a man reads a prepared speech, the listener unconsciously assumes that he has written down every little thing he knows about his subject—especially since the listener of course is no judge of the length of time he spent on it.

The extemporaneous speaker therefore always seems to draw from wide knowledge, while the manuscript reader seems to have exhausted his information in preparing his talk. *A good speaker should never confine himself to a manuscript.*

When a speaker prepares and uses a manuscript, it is because he is afraid of getting stuck in his speech. This fear may be caused by sheer stage fright, or by apprehension of forgetting the speech with a consequent total loss of memory.

I shall come back to stage fright in another connection later. For the present I would like to deal with the second possibility—fear of having one's memory go blank—and try to help the speaker who does not trust his memory.

CHAPTER XXV

PREPARING PUBLIC ADDRESSES

A METHOD for delivering a speech extemporaneously, without a manuscript, is of little use to those of my readers who do not know how to set about preparing the speech. That, too, must be studied. As preparing the speech is a necessary preliminary to delivering it in public, I shall give a few simple suggestions for guidance.

A definite, comprehensive **outline** of all your material is essential for every public address. It is not bad pedagogy for the school teacher to require that all compositions be first outlined. Although written essays and extemporaneous speeches differ in many respects, they have this in common: both must be **logically organised**.

In order to plan and outline an address, the speaker must review all the material he has on his subject. Therefore if a man is called on to speak on a subject about which he is not well informed, he must begin by **collecting and collating his material**; that is, he must connect his material with familiar **cue words** or with cues he conceived for this particular address. Not until he has collected and sifted his material can he set up an outline, for he must so frame his outline that he can put all his material under the different headings.

In addresses intended to be not only instructive but also persuasive to the speaker's point of view, it is essential to work out the end of the speech first. Since the correct ending is a condensed summary of the entire main theme of the address, it should therefore include the essential thoughts. So by carefully preparing a conclusion, the speaker can easily extract and put together leading sentences which at the same time serve as the skeleton of the entire speech.

In laying out his plan and **outlining** his material under the various **subheads**, the speaker must always keep the aim and purpose of his address in mind, the time allotted him, the place and the composition of the audience.

He must be especially clear in mind about the **aim and purpose of his speech**, so that he will **not** introduce ideas theoretically bearing upon his subject but **extraneous to the expressed purpose** of this particular address.

In a good speech no sentence and, of course, no paragraph is superfluous. Therefore the speaker should ask at every point of his talk, **Of what value is this to the subject as a whole**? and, Is it necessary and requisite for the deductions which the listener is to make from the address?

And the speaker must consider these points in reference to the **time allotted** him. If it is not definitely specified (as in a college lecture), the speaker must bear in mind that an **audience grows restive** at the most interesting of addresses.

Listening intently is a form of mental labour, and the more closely a person concentrates in listening to an address, the more he taxes his brain. The listener in most instances is learning something new, and as a consequence his brain works along with the speaker's in that it has to assimilate the new in some way.

It is therefore inconsiderate and rather unwise for a speaker to take up too much audience time.

An address of a purely theoretical nature, not enlivened by lantern slides or demonstrations, must not last more than **45 to 60 minutes**. The speaker who has not had enough experience and practice to judge from his outline the length of time required for his address should therefore **try out his whole speech aloud**, at least once, on his intimates, talking at the tempo he will later use in public, in order to see how long it will take.

Nothing is more unfortunate than to have everyone, even the most ingenuous member of the audience, notice that the speaker is **running over his time**. Everyone notices then that the speaker, while he is conscious of the fact that he should no longer try the patience of his audience, nevertheless cannot resist the temptation of crowding in all he can in a few minutes—perhaps really essential points. The result is a **feeling of nervous tension** on the part of speaker and audience. This tension grows and yet it could have been prevented by the simple means mentioned above.

The speaker who runs over his time often suffers further misfortune. Swayed by the feeling that he must soon bring his address to a close, he uses such expressions as "**In conclusion**," or the like, without having the following sentences bear out his statement.

He overlooks the fact that one should never promise his audience anything, not even the conclusion of a speech, without keeping his word. Such an occurrence allows the audience to ascribe **unreliability** to the lecturer. And they do not restrict it to the instance in question but extend it to the man's very personality and the contents of his address.

Along with a careful gauge of his allotted time the speaker must always take the **place** into consideration. The larger the hall, the slower must be his **speaking tempo**, in order that he may enunciate clearly and loudly enough to be heard in the last rows. Since one can speak much faster in a room, where the question of clear articulation is simple, than in a hall, the speaker must find out the size of the auditorium in advance in order to judge the time needed for his talk.

It is just as important, especially for the beginner, to consider **what kind of public** he will have before he prepares his speech. The degree of culture, the sex, and above all the factual knowledge must be considered in detail.

If a **doctor** gives a talk on a course of treatment to a group of his colleagues, his address will be entirely different from what it would be to a **lay audience**. In the latter instance he must avoid medical terminology or at least explain his terms, which he would of course assume his fellow practitioners knew. The same holds true for diagnosis, prescriptions, and the like. The explanation of medical terms, unnecessary and therefore superfluous in a group of doctors, is, however, necessary and essential in a group of laymen. It would be a mistake to explain terms to the former, an error to omit explanations to the latter.

In order to avoid unfortunate errors of this nature the speaker in preparing his address must bear the type of audience in mind. If he has a **mixed public**, professional people and laymen, it is necessary for him to turn from the one to the other as the occasion demands.

As another example: The lawyer who pleads his cases exclusively before learned judges will necessarily choose other words than for a speech before people not versed in law, as for instance a jury.

In the first case, he will lay most emphasis on a clear style and the decisions in like cases before the court; in the latter instance, he will bear in mind the human and psychological factors involved.

But the speaker must fit himself not only to the factual knowledge of the public but also to their **average education.**

In general one may say: Delight in independent thinking is measured by degree of culture. It is therefore a good idea for the speaker not to exhaust **all the details of his subject** and not to draw all the conclusions himself when he is addressing a cultured gathering. It is a better plan for him to give them the **foundation stones,** perhaps also the blue-print and plans, and let them build the mental structure themselves. But this treatment of his material is not advisable for a less cultured audience. Rather, it is necessary for him not only to introduce facts and examples, but even to draw the conclusions himself and explain them to his audience as clearly as he can.

But in any case the speaker should never exhaust his material and consequently land in a morass of **unrelated details**. Such an address easily loses all lucidity and bores the audience. It is also to his advantage and interest to present appropriate summaries showing that he is complete master of his subject, limited only by time and the mental capacity of the audience.

If the address calls for proofs or demonstrations, the speaker must be sure to make them general and understandable. There is no point in bolstering a statement with examples familiar to the speaker but unknown to a part of the audience. According to the degree of culture of the audience, the speaker must also make his basic statements before he develops them.

CHAPTER XXVI

*THE INTRODUCTION AND THE CONCLU-
SION OF A LECTURE*

IF I devote an entire section to the introduction and the conclusion of a lecture, it is because these two sections are so often neglected.

First of all, the introduction and the conclusion must be related to the main theme in the matter of time. In the usual 45- to 60-minute lecture, the introduction should not take more than about three minutes, and the conclusion perhaps five minutes.

The introductory remarks serve a twofold purpose: introducing the speaker personally and introducing his factual material.

The speaker must first establish a personal relationship with his audience, if he has had no introduction as guest speaker; in addition, he must tell the subject of his talk and his reason for speaking.

In speeches to clubs these two points are often appropriated by the chairman in his welcoming address. The speaker should therefore omit them from his introduction or restrict himself to a very few words on the subject. It is poor policy for him to repeat what the chairman has just stated in other words. This is a further argument against reading a speech from manuscript, for it is only the person accustomed to speaking extemporaneously who can at the last minute fit his opening remarks to the introductory words of the chairman.

If the speaker has been advertised, or if the occasion does not demand a personal introduction—as, for instance, a course in college—the subject should be defined at the outset. In doing so the speaker must remember that the public in most cases knows only the title of the lecture announced in the papers, on posters, or the like. Such a title, which is necessarily terse and rather commonplace, merely indicates the context without defining it. Very often the same title might apply to an entirely different aspect of the subject or a different treatment of it. But in a good lecture the introduction does not leave the listener in doubt about what subject, or rather what aspect of the subject, the lecturer will treat.

An exact definition of his theme is therefore the main point of the factual part of the introduction.

If, in his rather trite title and commonplace announcements, the speaker cannot avoid using a foreign word or a term not commonly known—such as "mnemotechny"—it is his duty to define it as clearly as he can in his introduction.

If the subject itself is difficult to explain, as for instance a theoretical topic demanding experiments and illustrations, it is permissible and advisable, at the end of the introduction, to sketch a plan of the entire lecture and to tell the audience what they may expect.

There is an advantage to this technique in that the auditor can come to a halt at the various stopping places along with the lecturer, and therefore be in a better position to concentrate.

One uses somewhat the same principle when taking a child for a walk. As modern psychology has long since recognised, one should never set out with the child without a plan of action. A distinct goal is necessary and, if possible, stopping places along the way in order that the child may take pleasure in the walk and not find it tedious.

The *conclusion* of a speech is even more important than the introduction. The speaker must always remember that his concluding words make the *most lasting impression* and must therefore be exact and definite.

The conclusion has the task of summarising the topic sentences of the main theme and impressing them on the listener, not to say hammering them home if he has not followed the discourse attentively.

The word "summarising" of course does not mean a detailed repetition of statements previously made, since they weary and bore the listener. Merely the most important thoughts in condensed form should and must be repeated in the conclusion. That is, the words "I approach the end of my discourse" or "I summarise briefly" are entirely permissible and customary. In fact, they are to be recommended, since the listener, from experience, pays renewed attention to the words which follow—an attention comparable to the tension he experiences at the end of a prize fight. He knows *that the most important things will follow*—the conclusions drawn from the preceding lines of thought. He knows, also, that the end of the lecture is definitely at hand, and he will therefore *concentrate his attention*, if the speaker has been able to catch it at all, on the matter in hand.

Since the conclusion should be memorable, it is often desirable to enliven it with a suitable visual image, a quotation, or a proverb.

The average man is inclined to accept a familiar quotation or a proverb as true. If the speaker is fortunate enough to tie up his deductions with a quotation or a proverb, so that the combination makes an impression on his listeners, they are often inclined to transfer the accuracy of the quotation to the contents of the speech itself. Of course, such an association should be handled with care; that is, proverbs and quotations must not be dragged in willy-nilly, but must come in quite naturally and easily if they are to make the intended impression.

What astonishing after-effects clear-cut and cleverly fashioned closing sentences can have is best shown by the fact that such words persist not only for decades but for centuries. As a case in point, think of Cato's remark, familiar to all school children who learn Latin:

"Delenda est Carthago!"

Notes for a Lecture

Our advice in regard to talking without a manuscript does not imply that the beginner should deny himself every kind of written aid.

We have already discussed the excellent impression made by the man who can speak entirely extemporaneously and we know that we can call the chain method to our aid in order to cultivate the art ourselves.

But since we are proceeding step by step in this book, we shall first discuss the ways and means available to the beginner in freeing himself from the written speech on the one hand and keeping to written cues on the other.

These cues are usually called lecture notes. These are made to ensure the speaker against getting stuck in passing from one train of thought to another, but they may claim his eye for only a split second at a time, for he must not let it stray from his audience for any length of time.

It follows that lecture notes should never consist of complete sentences, but only cues which can be read at a glance and yet suffice in connecting one thought with another. These cues should refer to the most important thoughts in the lecture, so that no essential point will be overlooked. It is not practical to list the *cue words* one under the other. It is better to *write them down in a rather pictorial fashion so that they catch the eye.*

Experiments have proved the majority of mankind to be eye-minded—to remember the pictorial best. If the cues are arranged pictorially their individual positions on the paper are unconsciously impressed on the mind through repeated reading, and the speaker need not, during the course of his speech, search for the cue to his talk at that point. For this reason notes should not be written down at the last minute, but as soon as the speaker has decided what plan he will use in his treatment of the subject.

Then, as he develops his speech, he should lay aside his cue sheet and, at first silently but later aloud, memorise his train of thought with the aid of his notes. If, with the help of his cues and the vocabulary at his command, he is able to develop his thoughts and express them clearly in good style, he may rest assured that his ability to do so will not desert him at the critical moment of facing his audience.

And let the beginner take heart in the fact that there is scarcely a speaker who does not lose the thread of his discourse in the course of a rather lengthy lecture. No matter how disciplined his powers of concentration, he will wander from his subject to some degree during the course of his talk, either through some remark from the audience, the opening and closing of a door, or even some vagrant thought of his own.

For the beginner, losing the thread of his discourse is the same as getting stuck. The experienced lecturer, if he does not immediately get back to his subject, will repeat his last statement in other words and meanwhile glance at the next phrase on his cue sheet, assuming he has a picture of his notes sufficiently clear in mind to know which cue was last used and about where on the sheet the next one will be.

It is not a bad policy for a speaker who has "run off the rails" in this way to develop a point more tersely than he had intended. It is even advisable to return to the point later on and add what was omitted, provided naturally that the speaker has not progressed beyond this division of his talk. If he has, he should pass it by, for if he does not he will make his address more involved for the audience.

The lecturer should always take into account the fact that his public knows *the plan* of his address or at least can grasp it, but that it never knows *in what way* he will develop his subject-matter under the various headings. Therefore he can make certain transpositions and changes in his original plans about which his audience does not know, so long as he does not disturb his main outline.

The same holds true for a not uncommon occurrence: the speaker suddenly gets a new idea while delivering his lecture, an idea he would like to incorporate. Such additions are possible if the new idea crops up during the discussion of the section in which it properly belongs. But if it appears as an afterthought, the speaker should not recapitulate and go back to a section in order to bring it in. This would do his lecture more harm than good. There is scarcely a single thought so essential as to justify disturbing the entire plan of a lecture for its inclusion.

Although we have referred quite generally to *the* cue sheet, we do not mean that *one and only one* sheet is permissible. But it is a good idea when you use several sheets of paper to use a small size, to write on only one side of the paper, and to clip the sheets together, so that one or more will not be misplaced during the lecture or slide from the stand or the table to the floor.

Bending down to pick them up causes hilarity, breaks the contact between speaker and audience, and in general ruins the lecture.

CHAPTER XXVII

A PRACTICAL EXAMPLE OF A CUE SHEET

As an illustration of what an actual cue sheet looks like, I have chosen Chapter XXV of this book, the chapter on "Preparing Public Addresses." The cue sheet for this section might read as follows:

Outline
  logically organised
    collecting and collating material
      cue words
        outlining under subheads
           Aim and purpose of the speech
             not extraneous to the expressed purpose
               Of what value is this to the subject as a whole?
      Time allotted
        audience grows restive
        45 to 60 minutes
          try out the whole speech aloud
Running over the time
  feeling of nervous tension
    "In conclusion"   *Place*
    unreliability   speaking tempo
What kind of public
  Example: doctor   *Average education*
    lay audience   all details of the subject
    mixed public   foundation stones
                    unrelated details

In order to follow these cues more easily, turn back to

Chapter XXV. You will find that those words—and only those—written on the cue sheet are in boldface type.

Now, practise the following exercise: Read and re-read the section on "Preparing Public Addresses" until you know its contents rather well.

Then turn back to this cue sheet and with its aid try to recapitulate the section as closely as you can. Do this by yourself three or four times and then lay the book, open at the cues, on a table or desk and repeat the entire chapter-section *aloud*, aided by the cues, as though you were addressing a large gathering.

When you have progressed so far that you can repeat the contents without getting stuck and without losing the thread of your discourse, try making a public address on the subject to your family or friends. If there is someone in your group who can criticise your mode of expression and general style, by all means ask him to attend.

When you have mastered this address, choose a new subject and repeat the exercise; that is, follow the rules you used for Chapter XXV.

Collect and collate your material, make an outline, pay attention to all the other matters you heeded so successfully in your first attempt. Then write out a cue sheet, somewhat similar to the one given above, and with its aid make your address.

As a final step, link your cue words by using the chain method as shown in Chapter VII. In this way you will be able to make the longest and most difficult address extemporaneously, without notes, in any auditorium. You will not be encumbered with a scrap of paper; you will be able to look directly at your public, and therefore you can be confident of success.

But remember: A good lecture or address must not

only be logical in organisation and comprehensive in content, but also pleasing and clear-cut in speech. A varied vocabulary and a variety in sentence structure are especially important. So we shall consider these subjects now.

CHAPTER XXVIII

A VARIED VOCABULARY

THE speaker who is able to express himself without using hackneyed phrases, and who can inject colour into his talk by means of a variety of images and a well-rounded vocabulary, can feel fairly sure of holding the attention of his audience, for it will not become apathetic from the boring conviction of knowing what is coming next.

There are few things which bore an audience more and make a lecture more thoroughly monotonous than the constant repetition of words.

An address is always more effective if the speaker can vary his vocabulary as well as his sentence structure. The good speaker employs a vocabulary of 10,000 to 15,000 words, whereas the average vocabulary embraces only 2,000 or 3,000 words. The other terms either are theoretically familiar to the student of public speaking but not freely used, or else they remain unknown to him.

In order to enrich his vocabulary he should pay attention to unfamiliar words when he runs across them in books or newspapers or in his attendance at lectures, and even in his daily intercourse.

He should impress them on his mind and, if need be, write them down. He should, as a further step, accustom himself gradually to use them and so in time widen his vocabulary. But if he reads or hears words whose meanings he does not know, he should never neglect looking them up in a dictionary or an encyclopedia. He must recognise the fact that the more words he has at his command the more fluently and effectively he will speak, but he must be sure that he knows a word before he uses it. This holds for foreign words as well as for the less familiar words in his native language.

The feeling for words can be sharpened and a vocabulary extended by collecting synonyms and determining what essential difference there is between them.

The words *speak, tell, say, relate, narrate,* like the words *chapter, part, subdivision, unit, section,* mean practically the same, but there is always a subtle distinction between any two of them.

The beginner should try to make these distinctions very clear. To do this, let me repeat my advice: Always do these exercises *aloud instead of silently,* in order to approach your goal more closely.

Defining words is an excellent habit for anyone who wants to widen his vocabulary and practise speaking in public. As long as concrete objects are selected for definition, the matter is comparatively simple, for anyone can define the meaning of house, garden, or table. It is, however, a little more difficult where abstract ideas are concerned, and the questions, What is humour? What is pride? What is self-defence? are not so easy to answer concisely in one sentence.

In formulating the answer special attention must be paid to having the definition not only exact but so precise that it cannot apply to all sorts of other things.

And the speaker is often forced to employ foreign terms or difficult concepts out of context. I have already discussed the fact that an address to laymen must be treated differently from the one to professionals.

Statements of fact which may be assumed to be familiar to colleagues must be explained thoroughly to laymen either in their own terms or in synonyms. The making of such substitutions belongs to the task of the student of speech.

If he has accustomed himself to defining concrete and abstract terms effortlessly and clearly, he can go a step further and attempt quotations and proverbs. Such practice is worthy of emulation because *it helps to develop quick thinking* and the rapid and precise gathering and outlining of material.

Variety in Sentence Structure

Next to a varied vocabulary, variety in sentence structure is important in preventing monotony, in heightening dramatic effect, and giving the voice an opportunity to change its tone or rhythm. The beginner often is at fault in this respect. He goes to one of two extremes.

One speaker places one declarative sentence after another without daring to use questions, subordinate clauses, or declamatory statements. Such a person might begin a lecture on Paris as follows: "Paris is one hour by air from London. It is divided into twenty *arrondisse-ments*. The heart of Paris is the Ile de la Cité. On the Ile de la Cité stands Notre-Dame. Paris has been called *la ville lumière*. The Métro is the Paris underground railway. The Place Pigalle is famous for its night life. There are many historic buildings in Paris. They include the Madeleine, the Panthéon, the Arc de Triomphe, the Hôtel de Ville, the Palais-Bourbon. . . ." Such a monotonous use of the declarative sentence is, of course, deadly.

Another speaker, wishing to avoid this monotony, becomes so involved in explanatory phrases without point or conclusion, that he cannot disentangle himself. This is equally undesirable.

The good speaker must avoid periodic sentences which are too long, but must utilise all possibilities of the language, such as declamatory sentences, rhetorical questions, and a variety of subsidiary clauses, in order to give his speech colour and variety. For this purpose, practice in everyday speech, in all manner of expression, is admirable.

Example of a simple *declarative sentence:* Industry prospers more when the people are convinced that peace is assured for a number of years.

The same in the form of an *exclamatory sentence:* May the people be convinced that peace is assured for a number of years, in order that industry may prosper!

Direct question: How will the conviction that peace is assured for a number of years affect the people? Industry will prosper.

Rhetorical question: Will the conviction of the people that peace is assured for a number of years have an effect on industry?

Repetition of the original declaratory sentence, in inverse order: The more the people are convinced that peace is assured for a number of years, the more industry will prosper!

Such variations are indispensable to the speaker. During an address itself there is no time to indulge in lengthy meditation and gauge which form will be most effective.

It is therefore necessary to cultivate the different forms of expression through practice in daily conversation, observing, as you do so, how each affects the listener.

Pay particular attention to the questions. The cited examples of direct and rhetorical questions differ in their effects: The direct question demands an answer which the speaker usually supplies himself. The rhetorical question, on the contrary, carries an implied answer. But one must be on guard lest the *positive* rhetorical question be interpreted *negatively*, and vice versa.

If, for instance, in the sentence given above, the rhetorical question reads: Will the conviction of the people, that peace is assured for a period of years, *not* have a beneficial effect on industry? the speaker through the insertion of the negative *not* wants to assert that the conviction will have a beneficial effect. But when the speaker asks, "Is that fitting and proper?" he wishes to express through this positive form of the rhetorical question that the matter under discussion is *not* to be construed as fitting and proper.

CHAPTER XXIX

STAGE FRIGHT

Its Causes

EVEN complete mastery of one's subject and the finest delivery cannot assist the speaker overcome with stage fright.

By "stage fright" we mean the condition of unreasoning terror that assails certain speakers, actors or singers shortly before they are to appear before a gathering of people.

This affliction is particularly awkward if, instead of disappearing during the course of the performance, it remains present or even grows more pronounced. And, unfortunately, the good friends and acquaintances who kindly tell one not to be afraid are not only most ineffective but they often *increase rather than diminish* stage fright.

In order to combat this evil effectively we must first discover its roots, which vary in individual cases.

One of the most usual causes is *the fear of getting stuck*, regardless of whether the speaker is conscious of the fact or not. For this reason we find stage fright more common to the actor than to the lecturer, because the former has to memorise verbatim, while the latter can rely on his facility in speech and his knowledge of his subject, without necessarily knowing it word for word.

The man who is accustomed to speaking extemporaneously, who has had experience in speaking before small gatherings, has proved to himself his ability to clothe his thoughts unhesitatingly with the right words, and soon conquers his stage fright. The consciousness of being master of his material, combined with the certainty of being able to express his ideas forcefully, is enough to cure the public speaker of his shyness in large gatherings.

Another frequent cause of stage fright is *faulty breathing*. The beginner who, at a public address or even in a small gathering, has found himself unable to control his breathing and has had to gasp for air like a fish out of water, will fear a recurrence of this unpleasant dilemma. This fear will grow as the hour of his appearance comes nearer, and in this instance, too, kindly admonitions will avail little.

This evil can be combated only by regular and frequent exercises in breath control. The beginner should not appear in public until he has learned how to conserve his breath so that he no longer need fear constriction in his throat.

Once he is consciously able to conserve and use his lungs and larynx in accordance with the demands of his sentence structure, his feeling of apprehension will disappear of itself and a rather important cause of stage fright will have been removed.

But the most common cause of stage fright is simply *fear of appearing before a crowd*. Persons who are able to talk fluently when conversing tête-à-tête and who are not awkward in small gatherings or at large dinner-parties are assailed by sudden fear when they have to address an impersonal audience. The main reason for this state lies in overvaluing the critical capacities of the crowd.

The beginner believes that everything he says must be particularly weighty because he is talking to a larger, more critical gathering. And yet it should be obvious to him that the very reverse is true; the critical capacity of the crowd is inferior to that of the individual.

In a rather large audience the individual is easily inclined to leave criticism to others. The speaker who has prepared his speech carefully and is thoroughly familiar with his material naturally knows more about his subject than the listener who attends in order to learn something new. When the student of public speaking realises this fact, his exaggerated fear of criticism from the crowd disappears. No trace of stage fright will remain when he is once convinced that he has something of real factual importance to impart to his audience.

For practice I can merely advise you to *increase the size of your audience gradually*. That is, first give your talk, thoroughly prepared and outlined on a cue sheet, to friends and acquaintances, and do not step before the public until you have tried out your speech on a small and select group. But in the final analysis, we must repeat, stage fright cannot be cured by simple, logical reasoning. It is an emotion buried in the subconscious mind. It has all the earmarks of what we call an inferiority complex, which we must combat with all the means at our disposal, since it reacts on man's achievements and ultimate success.

Thanks to the researches of Coué and Baudouin on the one hand, and Freud and Adler on the other, we know nowadays that the subconscious has a powerful effect on thought and action. It is merely necessary to apply the right method in guidance for each individual case.

Its Cure

Strange to relate, there are still some unenlightened people who do not believe in the subconscious mind because they can neither see, hear, smell, nor taste it.

What are dreams and what is their source? You are convinced that you "dream" in the true sense of the word only when you are sound asleep. Sleep, however, means the complete absence of conscious thought. But if, in spite of this complete lack of consciousness, you nevertheless see, hear, or experience anything at all, it is proof that something else exists beside or beneath actual consciousness.

No doubt you have often awakened in the morning with the lingering memory of a dream, yet unable to recall the content of your dream no matter how hard you try.

Shortly afterward you go out in the street and see something that calls back a fragment of your dream. At the same moment its entire content flashes into your memory.

Let us try to explain this peculiar occurrence. If we picture the subconscious as resting below the conscious mind of man, the two must be separated by a door which we can visualise as open or closed. The step leading to this door we designate the threshold of consciousness.

The dream and all that goes with it rest on the subconscious (if your sleep is sufficiently deep). But when anything—a person, animal, or object—enters the circle of your consciousness, tied up or *associated* with a similar thing in your subconscious mind, the connection can be strong enough to project the dream-content over the threshold of consciousness.

In everyday practical life, as well as in dreams, there is evidence of the existence of the subconscious. You must at some time or other have had the experience of being unable to recall a perfectly familiar name. It may be the name of an acquaintance, a place, or a foreign word.

In such instances, we are apt to use the expression: "The name's on the tip of my tongue," and explain that at the moment we cannot recall it. Since we knew this name a short while before and since we shall later recall it unaided, we have proof that it really is in our minds. But if we are unable, in spite of this fact, to recall it, momentarily it is not "known" to us; or in other words, besides our positive consciousness there must be another mental sphere, belonging to our consciousness but beyond our control. Since this other or second consciousness lies under the truly conscious we call it the subconscious.

The effect of the subconscious on your daily life cannot be rated too highly. Assume that somehow, somewhere you get to know a person whom you have never before seen. In most cases you immediately develop a *feeling of like or dislike*, that is, *sympathy or antipathy*.

There is no logical explanation for this feeling, since you have never heard anything about this person and consequently do not really know him. And his appearance may offer no grounds or excuse for your feeling. The use of the term "feeling" is sufficient proof of the fact that there is *no logical explanation* for your attitude.

Nowadays psychologists know that all feelings of this sort are based on the subconscious and that by psychoanalysis and hypnosis they can discover the subconscious reasons for them and make them "known." Psycho-analysis and hypnosis render one way of curing stage fright.

For the present we will be content with observing that *inferiority complexes* also have their roots in the subconscious and that *stage fright is merely a manifestation of a general feeling of inferiority*. What causes an inferiority complex? How can it be removed?

As far as causes are concerned, Individual Psychology

teaches us that the roots of an inferiority complex are found in childhood experiences.

The child is totally unable to fight the battle of life with his own weapons and in all cases relies on the help of adults. The more conscious a child is of his inadequacy and weakness, the greater is his feeling of inferiority. Child education should attack this feeling at the proper time. Unthinking parents and educators foster it in the child when they continually refer to his unimportance, insignificance and inferiority.

In many cases the child is made conscious of his general inadequacy by being required to do things which he cannot do and which should not be expected of him at his age.

How this general feeling of inferiority will develop depends upon the child. Many children consider themselves very important and their impulse is to take the centre of the stage and demand the undivided attention of their parents and educators. If they thrust themselves into the foreground merely to balance their own insignificance and feeling of inferiority, no harm is done.

Some time and somehow the child will of course learn to adapt himself to his environment. It may be in kindergarten, at play with children of his own age, or not until he goes to school, where the same demands are made of children of the same age-level.

The child who feels himself thrust into the background is the one who attempts to impress his superiority on his companions of like age or else tries to make them believe him superior. In this instance, we speak of an overcompensation of the feeling of inferiority. I need not emphasise the point that this is all a matter of unconscious behaviour, for it stands to reason that little ones or even school children are not acting consciously.

At any rate it is clear that a feeling of inferiority

almost always has its roots in false methods of child education. A feeling of inferiority is hardly ever innate, but is "suggested" to the child by ignorant parents and educators.

Fortunately we know that *every feeling called forth by suggestion can be removed by suggestion.* It is therefore not too difficult a task to find methods for removing stage fright and an inferiority complex.

But, we must remember, the man whose fear of the public is so great that he dare not make a speech even when he has something important to say, usually is the one who applies for a job in fear and trembling, utterly unable to tell what he knows in a rational manner.

These persons *must suggest to themselves* that they are perfectly capable of fighting their own battles and thereby remove the suggestion of inadequacy.

Naturally the simplest cure would be to achieve something so important that it would excite the admiration of one's fellows.

The admiration of one's own little world is the most effective means of convincing a person of his ability and knowledge, thereby choking off all feeling of inferiority. The difficulty in applying this remedy lies in the fact that people with inferiority complexes rarely can accomplish really great and unusual things as long as they suffer from this feeling.

How, then, are we going to overcome this sense of inferiority? *By mnemotechny!* The simplest experiment, that is, the repetition of a rather long series of words, will do the trick. Far-fetched, you think. But these mnemotechnical exercises, faithfully performed, are useful in facing the scoffer, because they work.

As you have already learned, they operate in twofold fashion. First of all, we know that mnemotechnical series of words strengthen one's powers of concentration remarkably. *Powers of concentration in turn foster self-assurance*, since they convince a man of his own knowledge and abilities. Self-assurance and a feeling of inferiority are, however, incompatible; where one gains the ascendancy the other must give way.

It should be easy to add a mastery of sentences to one's mastery of words. If the words are so chosen that they serve as cues for a unified address, anyone who can repeat them can also in a short time repeat a series of sentences related to them. If he has repeated the series of words not only aloud to himself but to a circle of friends and acquaintances as well, he will be able to do the same with sentences. In doing so he proves to his own satisfaction that he can make a public address. As soon as he realises this, his fear of speaking disappears.

A second factor enters in, which at first glance seems unrelated, but in reality is *extraordinarily important*. The experiment of being able to repeat out of sequence a rather long list of twenty or thirty words, after hearing them once, will *impress all* those who do not know the mnemotechnical connections.

If you have followed my advice you have long since had this experience. Arousing the interest and approval of a gathering is tantamount to applause and is a turning point in conquering feelings of inferiority, especially stage fright. Approbation strengthens one's self-assurance, and self-assurance and an inferiority complex are mutually antipathetic. Even the applause of a rather small circle is extraordinarily *suggestive*, and this power of suggestion increases with the size of the audience as well as with the repetition of the experiment.

As you see, these factors work on each other and *mnemotechnical aids are effective in transforming the shy, apprehensive person who fears an audience into a self-assured entertaining personality.*